The hymns of the Christian faith are an untapped treasury of devotional riches and spiritual nurture. *Hymn Workouts* invites us to open this storehouse. Among the book's most obvious virtues are the comprehensiveness of topics covered, the originality of the enterprise, and the multiplicity of ingredients that the author's creative mind has brought together in the individual entries. This is a one-of-a-kind book that opens the door to a richer spiritual life.

LELAND RYKEN
Emeritus Professor of English, Wheaton College, Wheaton, Illinois
Author of sixty books, including
40 Favorite Hymns on the Christian Life

This wonderful work takes the lyrics our hearts love to sing and pairs them with reflections that help our minds meditate deeply on the truths contained within. I trust the devotional aspects of the book will enliven its doxological heartbeat.

MATT BOSWELL
Pastor, The Trails Church; Hymnwriter; Assistant Professor of Church Music and Worship, The Southern Baptist Theological Seminary

Not only does this book help us rediscover the beauty and splendour of our God through the treasured hymns of the past, but it reconnects our weary hearts to a steady rhythm of Scripture that pumps life into the soul. As a music leader and pastor, I believe this will be a wonderful resource to help lift our eyes to Jesus and allow the beauty of God to be enjoyed daily. In a busy and hectic world, I appreciate more and more a study that helps me to slow down and enjoy the Saviour and His Word.

JASON NELSON
Pastor and Music Leader, 20Schemes

If you want to kindle your love for God, read this book. It is a steady flame that will reignite your candle of faith, set ablaze your torch of vision, and warm a cooling heart. How? Because its pages invite us to gaze at the eternal flames of glory Moses met in the desert. My soul already owes a debt to Barnard for writing it.

JORDAN LOFTIS
Bestselling author and president of Short Daily Devotions

Fitness doesn't happen by accident – physically or spiritually. In this book, Joe Barnard gives the equivalent of 100 spiritual WODs (workout of the day) that will stretch and challenge anyone willing to do them. These workouts are valuable in every respect (1 Tim. 4:8). Pick one up and get after it!

TYRELL HAAG
Senior Pastor, Pineland Baptist Church, Burlington, Ontario, Canada

HYMN

WORKOUTS

100 Exercises to Set Your Heart Ablaze

JOE BARNARD

CHRISTIAN
FOCUS

Copyright © Joe Barnard 2022

paperback ISBN 978-1-5271-0892-9
ebook ISBN 978-1-5271-0953-7

Published in 2022
by
Christian Focus Publications Ltd,
Geanies House, Fearn, Ross-shire,
IV20 1TW, Scotland, UK.
www.christianfocus.com

Cover design by Pete Barnsley

Printed by Bell and Bain, Glasgow

Contents

Introduction 11

Outline of Exercises 27

Section 1

Meditating on the Holiness of God 29

  1 Divine Transcendence 32

  2 The Incomprehensibility of God..........................34

  3 The Beauty of Holiness 36

  4 The Mystery of the Trinity 38

  5 The Eternity of God..40

  6 The Omnipotence of God.......................................42

  7 The Omnipresence and Omniscience
     of God 44

  8 The Faithfulness of God..46

  9 The Love of God 48

 10 The Majesty of God 50

Section 2

Meditating on the Mystery of the Gospel 53

 11 The Eternal Love of the Father...............................56

 12 The Eternal Love of the Son 58

 13 The Glory of God Incarnate....................................60

 14 The Incarnation Transforms Our Knowledge
     of God 62

 15 Christ: The Pattern of Perfection 64

16 The Miracles of Grace 66

17 The Cross Reveals the Awfulness of Sin 68

18 The Power of the Cross to Change Us 70

19 Tarrying beside the Cross 72

20 The Cross as a Personal Encounter 74

21 The Cross Is Always Before Us 76

22 The Cross as a Source of Revelation 78

23 The Resurrection: Christ's Victory over
Death 80

24 Living a Resurrected Life 82

25 The Glory of the Ascended King 84

26 The High Priestly Ministry of Christ 86

27 The Joy of Having a Perfect High Priest 88

28 The Sympathy of Our High Priest 90

29 All Authority Has Been Given to Christ 92

30 The Authority of Christ in the Salvation of
a Sinner 96

31 The Authority of Christ in the Sanctification of
a Christian 98

32 The Authority of Christ in the Salvation of
the Church 100

33 Preparing for the Judgment of Christ 102

34 The Dawning of the New Jerusalem 104

Section 3

Meditating on Spiritual Fellowship 107

35 The Glory of the Father 110

36 The Mercy of the Father 112

37 The Kindness of the Father 114

38 The Sheer Delight of Knowing the Father 116

39 Though We Have Not Seen Jesus, We Love Him 118

40 The Sweetness of Christ's Presence 120

41 Your Presence Makes My Paradise 122

42 Jesus, Thou Art All 124

43 To See Thee Is to Praise Thee 126

44 Communing with Jesus as High Priest 128

45 Fleeing to Jesus in Moments of Need 130

46 The Majesty of the Spirit 132

47 The Unique Gifts of the Spirit 134

48 The Spirit's Gift of Assurance 136

49 The Intimacy of Communion with the
   Holy Spirit 138

50 The Holy Spirit Inspires Worship 140

51 The Communion of Saints 142

52 Joint Pilgrims on the Road to Glory 144

53 Bond of Perfection 146

Section 4

Meditating on Spiritual Transformation 149

54 The Spiritual Power of Beauty 152

55 Love: Our Highest Motive 154

56 Teach Me to Love You More 156

57 The Giver Is Greater than the Gifts 158

58 Love Orders the Heart 160

59 From Duty to Choice 162

60 The Debt of Gratitude 164

61 The Joy of Indebtedness 166

62 Ten Thousand Reasons to Be Grateful 168

63 Submission 170

64 Yielding 172

65 Obedience 174

66 Self-Denial 176

67 Humility 178

68 Trust 180

69 Fortitude 182

70 Hope 184

71 Courage 186

72 Godly Fear...188

73 Joy 190

Section 5

Meditating on Spiritual Disciplines 193

74 The Spirit Must Illumine the Word 196

75 The Sanctifying Light of the Word 198

76 The Word Gives Us Life......................................200

77 Meditating on the Word Day and Night.............202

78 The Essence of Prayer 204

79 Stop Complaining; Start Praying........................206

80 Prayer Is Warfare...208

81 The Longing for Nearness to God 210

82 The Gift of a Broken Heart 212

83 Transparent Confession.......................................214

84 Christ, Our Sin Offering......................................216

85 The Passion for Purity..218

86 Fulfilling the Great Commission 220

87 Practicing the Presence of God in the
        Busyness of Life..222

88 Ordinary Life as a Spiritual Vocation.................224

89 Fulfilling the Great Commission 226

Section 6

Meditating on Spiritual Trials 229

90 Beneath a Frowning Providence.........................232

91 The Refining Fire of Affliction 234

92 Joy in the Midst of Anxiety 236

93 The World Is a Battlefield 238

94 Watch and Pray...240

95 How Firm a Foundation 242

96 To Live Is Christ, To Die Is Gain 244

97 Forever with the Lord 246

98   Death: The Last Battle 248

99   The Hope of Bodily Resurrection 250

100   The Land of Pure Delight 252

      Final Lap: The Joy of Eternal Life 254

I dedicate this book to my mom, Margot Barnard, who first taught me to appreciate poetry, and to Rod Olps, who modeled for me the spiritual discipline of meditating on hymns.

Introduction

Let's start with a problem: A lot of Christians hit a low ceiling of spiritual growth. Most of us have felt this frustration. For a while, especially at the start of our Christian journey, we feel as if, every day, God is unlocking a new chest in the treasuries of His grace. Character is being transformed. The horizons of knowledge are expanding. The wellsprings of the heart are like irrepressible geysers that spontaneously shoot forth praise and gratitude.

Yet, over time, the pace of growth begins to slacken – first, from a sprint to a gallop, then to a canter, then to a lumbering walk, and, finally, to a standstill. We keep reading our Bibles, but we begin to feel as if our understanding of them is no better than it was a year – or even a decade – before. The coals of devotion that once burned so brightly begin to look more like a pile of ashes than a pile of embers. Spiritual disciplines grow stale. Routines harden into ruts. Eventually, the Christian life starts to feel a little bit like the process of aging. Our deepest ambition is no longer to continue the course of maturing, but just to hang on as long as we can to whatever vitality lingers in our deteriorating bones.

It's easy to become resigned to this condition. We look around and see that other Christians have the same struggles that we do. Thus, we conclude that treading water is the basic rhythm of the Christian life. We look to Numbers, not to Joshua, to frame our spiritual expectations. There is no conquest to be had in this life. There is no forward progress. Life has become just one big waiting room in which the believer is told to sit patiently until God finally calls our name and takes us home.

Now, in some respects, camping in the wilderness is a legitimate description of the Christian life. Each Christian is not called to be a Hercules, an exceptional hero who exhausts his life completing one heroic feat after another. Elizabeth Elliot, the missionary and author, once commented in an interview, that even among the frontier missionaries in the Amazon, most of life is filled, not with sensational acts of witness and mercy, but with dishes washed, floors swept, and dinners made.

And yet, admitting this, we need to be careful not to be *too* accepting of stagnating faith. There is an ever-present danger of using spiritual causes to explain natural phenomena. There are seasons when a quiet time feels arid due to a drought of joy that God mysteriously permits. Yet, other times, the problem is something far more mundane. A basic fact of human nature is that all of us hate discomfort. If faced with two options, one to go uphill and to try something new and another to glide downhill along a familiar path, most of us will choose the gentle downward slope whenever possible.

We need to recognize that this 'bias toward ease' is a spiritual liability. It's not hard to fall into a cycle in which a 'quiet time' is nothing more than a moment to snuggle up with God under a blanket with a mug of coffee in hand.

While there is nothing wrong with savoring the presence of God in a relaxed position, it should be pointed out that spiritual disciplines share a lot in common with physical exercise. In the world of fitness, the comfortable routine is rarely – if ever – the one that yields significant results. If a person is comfortable with jogging a mile and decides to go out and run a mile at the same casual pace every day, he may maintain the status quo, but he will never increase his stamina or improve his strength. Something similar is often true spiritually. If, each morning, a Christian wakes up and reads one chapter of Proverbs and then spends a few distracted minutes in prayer, he should expect the output of this routine to reflect the input. We all need to be honest enough to admit that a lot of what passes for a 'devotion' is more along the lines of a survival ration than a hearty diet for spiritual growth.

Does any of this sound familiar? If so, keep reading. This is a book for people whose spiritual routines are every bit as novel and exciting as doing laps on a hamster wheel.

This Book Is More Than a Devotional

At first glance, it would be tempting to label this book a devotional. It does indeed bear some resemblance to other collections of hymns and Psalms that have been gathered and arranged for spiritual nourishment. However, to call this book a devotional would be like mistaking a visit to a local CrossFit gym for a quiet morning in the library. The mere mention of 'devotional' conjures up all of the mental and physical habits that this book is designed to disrupt – passive reading, disengaged minds, glazed eyes, slumped posture, knitted blankets, and so on. The purpose of this book is not to provide a daily cup of warm chicken soup for the soul. This is a book of spiritual workouts that are meant to push complacent souls back out into the space of exertion and discovery. In fact, if taken as a whole, we might liken this book to a spiritual boot camp. It is intended to engage and sharpen the faculties of the mind (memory, imagination, intellect, conscience, and will) which, if left untended, are in danger of rusting to the point of being of little practical use.

The exercises in this book are based on an assortment of classic hymns.[1] For many readers, the mere mention of *hymn* will be enough to trigger a yawn. We should not be deceived by our assumptions. Though the hymns gathered here are old, they are not decrepit. Distilled within them is a purity of thought and passion that is wonderfully explosive. In fact, I will go further and say that there ought to be a warning label that goes along with these hymns. They are for the soul what gasoline is for an internal combustion engine. While contemplating them, all a reader needs is the faintest spark provided by the Holy Spirit, and suddenly, the pistons of the heart will churn with renewed drive to go out and climb the lofty roads of godliness.

No doubt, some will be skeptical of such claims. Is it really possible that an 18th century hymn by Charles Wesley can ignite the devotion of a 21st century Christian? The answer is not 'Maybe' but absolutely 'Yes'! Anyone hesitant to believe this claim needs to consider the following benefits that will come through an earnest engagement with the exercises in this book.

---

1   Perhaps the closest analogue to this book is J. C. Ryle's *Spiritual Songs: Being One Hundred Hymns Not to Be Found in the Hymn Books Commonly Used*, first published in 1868.

1 – You Will Experience the Power of Meditation

In modern schools we are taught that reading is a passive activity. The goal of reading has more to do with the dopamine hit of turning a page than it is about understanding the ideas that words and sentences are meant to communicate. Thus, it is not uncommon, for example, after reading a chapter of the Bible, for a person to have no memory at all of what has just been read. Technically, the eyes have scanned the words on a page, but the mind never alighted anywhere long enough to comprehend – much less retain – what was read.

Now, the best remedy for such mental flightiness is the practice of meditation. Isaac Watts, a polymath of the 18th century who also happens to be the greatest of English hymn writers, makes this point in *The Improvement of the Mind*. He says, 'As a man may be eating all day, and, for want of digestion is never nourished; so those endless readers may cram themselves in vain with intellectual food, and without real improvement of their minds, for want of digesting it by proper reflections.'[2] The point to glean from this remark is that reading without reflection is like eating without digestion. Minimal nourishment will be gained from a daily reading plan if we are unwilling to exert the effort required to process, organize, and store what has been consumed.[3]

This is where old hymns can be such useful training. Hymns are a form of poetry, and poetry is an attempt to sculpt thought into a simple and beautiful shape. To read

---

2   See Isaac Watts, *The Improvement of the Mind*, digital copies available online.

3   Psalm 1 is brutally honest about the point. According to the Psalm, there are only two types of people: Some are like firmly rooted trees, and others are like chaff blown about by the wind. What is the difference? Meditating.

a poem is a very different experience from reading a novel or a newspaper. For good reason, we often refer to novels as page-turners. The objective of reading such books is to speed along the highway of action as fast as possible so that we can observe a final scene. The objective of poetry is the opposite of this. A poem is like an empty bench along a scenic road. The point of reading poetry is to pause from the flurry of activity long enough so that we can appreciate a vista that otherwise would be missed. Thus, for a generation that is allergic to sustained thought, no exercise is more potent than taking the time to reflect on something like a hymn. This activity isolates atrophied muscles of the mind that are in desperate need of a strenuous work out.

Anyone reluctant to expend the energy required to meditate needs to listen to the testimony of eminent Christians who have gone before us. The great Puritan Thomas Brooks, much beloved by Charles Spurgeon, once wrote, 'It is not he who reads most – but he who meditates most, who will prove the choicest, sweetest, wisest and strongest Christian.'[1] These words should shock us. According to Brooks, the strength of a Christian has less to do with how many pages are covered in a year than how deeply truth is imprinted on the soul. Truth is not a pill that can be swallowed whole. For truth to enter our bloodstream and reach the heart, it needs to be broken down into bite-sized pieces and given time to dissolve in the mind.

---

1   See Thomas Brooks, *Precious Remedies for Satan's Devices*, 'To the Reader.' Countless other similar quotations could be added from the early church fathers, medieval doctors, and theologians in the reformed tradition. On this topic, the whole of the church is united. Meditation is essential for spiritual growth.

2 – *You Will Get a Thorough Education in Systematic and Practical Theology*

Modern Christians are unaware of the breadth of traditional hymn writing. Most contemporary praise has a very narrow focus. We either sing about the death and resurrection of Jesus, or about the invitation to accept the message of the gospel, or about the therapeutic benefits of faith and hope. While these topics are of undeniable importance, it is worth pointing out that traditionally Christians have sung praise about the whole gamut of the Christian life. There are hymns that cover every spiritual topic imaginable, ranging from specific attributes of God, to the various roles and offices performed by Christ, to focused treatment of individual spiritual disciplines, to beautiful descriptions of mature Christian character. In light of this, it is no exaggeration to claim that a comprehensive theological education can be attained merely by reading and studying hymns.[2] If there is a topic pertinent to the Christian life, be assured: at some point a faithful believer has mapped the location and published his findings in a short and memorable set of verses.

Yet, this raises a question: if hymns cover the same topics as spiritual books, why not just read books instead of study hymns? Here, two thoughts are worth considering.

First, hymns are concise. If someone is a natural reader, then, yes, by all means, there is no reason *not* to go out

---

2   John Wesley is famous for recommending hymns to disciple children. He wrote in the preface of the 1790 edition of *Hymns for Children*, 'The following hymns contain strong and manly sense, yet expressed in such plain and easy language as even children may understand. But when they do understand them, they will be children no longer, only in years and in stature.' The hymns in this book have a similar power: they can grow up spiritual children into manly followers of Christ.

and read hundreds of pages of dense theology in order to fill out a spiritual education. Yet, not everyone is built this way. In exercise, there is something called a 'HIIT' workout. The acronym stands for 'high intensity, interval training.' The idea is that, if invested with sufficient focus and exertion, a fifteen minute sprint workout can yield the same benefits as an hour of relaxed jogging on a treadmill. Personally, I am convinced that something similar is true for theological study. The marvel of a classic hymn is that it is able to concentrate scores of pages of reflection into a handful of unforgettable lines. For this reason, hymns are a perfect solution for people who struggle either to find time to read big books or who get little pleasure from the act of reading. Meditating on a hymn is a HIIT workout for the soul.

Second, one of the difficulties of studying theology is learning how to bridge the gap between the lofty ideas discussed by theologians and the ground-level struggles of normal life. Hymns are a natural bridge between truth and practice. The vast majority of them have been birthed out of the joys and struggles of the lives of ordinary believers who have had to wrestle with the promises of God in the trenches of a fallen world. This means that hymns are a ready form of applied theology. They are simple, but profound statements of faith, intended to feed worship and inspire courage in the dangerous – yet familiar – arena of struggle, affliction, temptation, and doubt.

3 – The Scriptures Will Come to Life with Beauty and Power

Classic hymns are tapestries of Scripture. In the case of great writers like Charles Wesley, John Newton, Isaac

Watts, Augustus Toplady, and William Cowper, almost every line of a hymn is either a direct quotation or an indirect allusion to the Bible. Thus, classic hymns are a unique way to explore the Bible itself. Very often, a hymn will take a theme like suffering and weave together various threads of the Old and New Testaments in order to show what faith looks like in the midst of affliction. This means that a hymn can be used as a spiritual basecamp. It gives the mind a fixed location from which different trails in the Scriptures can be explored, all converging at a common point.

This structure is not just good for the soul; it is also good for the mind. People who study the process of learning talk about the importance of clustering knowledge.[1] The mind is far better at retaining information that is presented in patterns than it is at storing free-standing ideas that are detached from any preexisting network of thought. A great hymn is a useful means of creating a new cluster of ideas centering on a Biblical theme. For example, by reading a hymn on the role of the Holy Spirit, and then exploring all of the references in the hymn to John's gospel and to Paul's epistles, a person will have a much better chance at engaging in what is called 'deep learning' than if he simply read a few pages of a book. The process of connecting ideas and seeing patterns will both enlighten the mind and fortify the memory.

Yet, there is a further spiritual benefit to meditating on great hymns. Hymns have a way of framing Biblical truths in a fresh and dynamic setting so that the familiar

---

1   For more on this see Richard Ogle, *Smart World: Breakthrough Creativity and the New Science of Ideas* (Boston: Harvard Business School Press, 2007) and Scott H. Young, *Ultralearning: Accelerate Your Career, Master Hard Skills and Outsmart the Competition* (London: Thorsons, 2019).

is felt to be new, and the old is made unforgettable. As evidence, consider an example. By the time a person has been a Christian for a handful of years, he will have heard the story of Jesus calming the storm countless times. If he is not careful, eventually, when the story comes up in a morning reading or Sunday sermon, familiarity will breed contempt. Eyes will gloss over, due to the feeling that there is nothing new to be seen.

Hymns are a protection against such spiritual numbness. Case in point, read the following stanza from one of Charles Wesley's hymns, which takes up the story of Jesus' miracle and applies it in an unexpected way:

When darkness intercepts the skies
And sorrow's waves around me roll,
When high the storms of passion rise,
And half o'erwhelm my sinking soul;
My soul a sudden calm shall feel,
And hear a whisper: Peace, be still!

This stanza invites the reader, not only to reflect on the extraordinary power of Christ, but to experience this power at a time of spiritual crisis. For example, note the way in which the story of the calming of the sea is recast from a physical miracle to a psychological one. In the hymn, darkness is not referring to the effect that clouds have when they block sunlight. Darkness describes the condition of the soul in a time of anxiety, grief, and fear – a moment in which the rays of God's loving presence are blocked by the pain of tumultuous circumstances. Similarly, the imagery of the storm and the waves become symbols of raging emotions in the heart. The picture is not one of a boat under threat of sinking, but of a soul that has reached a breaking point. And it is here that

Christ's words 'Peace, be still' (Mark 4:39) receive fresh application. Memory is an invitation to hope. The voice that once quieted a Galilean storm is understood to be a living Savior, who can still bring peace to a heart at the tipping point of despair.

Such is the power of hymns. They illumine the Scriptures by closing the gap between the past and the present and by unveiling a universal relevance to stories and promises, which, like manna, must be collected and consumed afresh each day.

4 – You Will Be Given Words to Express the Hidden Depths of Your Soul

What would it be like to see the beauty of creation through the eyes of an artist like Michelangelo or Rembrandt? What colors and shapes, textures and scenes would pop into view that otherwise might appear too mundane to be noteworthy? Or what would it be like to listen to the chatter of birds or to the murmur of a mountain brook with the ears of Bach or of Mozart? No doubt, the experience would be like stepping from a two-dimensional world into one with three dimensions. Beauty would come to life with an astonishing presence.

Similar questions can be asked of spiritual giants. What would it be like to long for God with the panting heart of Paul Gerhardt? What does the cross look like through the eyes of John Wesley? What does gratitude feel like in the soul of Robert Murray M'Cheyne? Such questions may appear to be nothing more than tantalizing thought-experiments. Yet, there is a way of stepping into the affective life of these men and getting at least a taste of their devotion. All of the Christians mentioned above deposited some of their most refined thoughts and feelings in hymns. To take up a hymn on the cross by Paul Gerhardt, for example, is an opportunity to dress up in the faith of this remarkable man. The point of the exercise is not to pretend to be something more than we are. The goal, rather, is to fan the dying embers of the heart. It is far too easy to settle in the Christian life. We stick to the foothills because we forget that there are higher mountains behind them. To read a great hymn is to be reminded of 'the much more' of the Christian life. We realize that we have not yet comprehended with all the saints what is 'the breadth and length and height and depth' (Eph. 3:18) of knowing God.

Yet, in truth, a great hymn does something even more important than expanding the horizons of devotion. The most potent of hymns has a unique ability to put into words what, for most of us, would otherwise be inexpressible. We find language that is suitable for the deepest groaning of the heart. And in this way, hymns become a script for personal devotion. They channel spiritual passions so that the heart can flow freely in praise and adoration.

How to Maximize the Benefits of This Book

Christian writers routinely follow a defunct recipe used by books on diet and fitness. They begin with theory and end with practice. It is no exaggeration to say that the vast majority of health and wellness books can be boiled down to some variant of the following formula: diet + exercise = fitness. In spite of popularity, this recipe is grievously inadequate. The basic formula for fitness is not diet + exercise = fitness but *character* + diet + exercise = fitness. When it comes to any form of exercise, there is no way of deleting the person from the plan without compromising the product. If a man or woman is serious about improving fitness, then discipline, self-control, perseverance, and optimism will be every bit as important as reducing sugar consumption and toning muscles. Without the right character, a plan will be of no more use than an appliance without electricity.

The same is true for this book. There is no substitute for the heart that a person brings to each of these exercises. As was mentioned already, output will reflect input. Two people can go through the same motions on a rowing machine, but get entirely different results. Similarly, two Christians can read the same hymns in this book and have entirely different experiences. What will make the difference? The answer is focus, attention, inquisitiveness, study, and, yes – *last because it is most important* – prayer.

In view of this, the place to begin with these exercises is not just a state of mind, but a state of body. As military drill sergeants understand, posture reflects attitude. Slouching lends itself to carelessness. A slumped back produces a slumped mind. For us, this means that there are two positions in which the following devotional activities can be performed. The very best option is on one's knees. Nothing induces a spirit of reverent prayer better than kneeling before God. The second best option is sitting at a desk with a Bible open, a notebook nearby, and a sharpened pencil in hand. Such an environment will signal to the mind that a serious activity is about to begin.

Now, each of the hymns should be viewed as an independent spiritual exercise. Although they are arranged topically, the idea is to complete one exercise each day. Remember, speed is not a virtue when it comes to meditation. It is far more beneficial to move slowly with comprehension and prayerfulness than to trample through multiple hymns like a child running through a flowerbed.

Likewise, each of these hymns should be viewed as a single exercise that involves multiple steps. In weight lifting, a clean and jerk cannot be performed properly unless each piece of the motion is completed correctly. The same is true here. Reading a hymn should not be mistaken for performing a spiritual exercise. To complete an exercise properly, four steps must be carefully followed.

Step 1: Observe the title at the top of the page and read the recommended Bible passage. This information will prime the mind for the subject matter of the hymn. A fast way to get injured during intense physical activity is to start sprinting around like a child without warming up. Although the stakes are different here, a similar blunder will be made if we jump into a hymn without any preparation. The title and reading will get the blood of worship circulating in the soul.

Step 2: Read slowly through the hymn, start to finish. It is important that in this reading you do not pause to figure out the meaning of the hymn. The forest needs to be seen before individual trees are identified and studied. If possible, read the hymn aloud. Poetry is not just meant to be thought; it is meant to be heard. The more senses that get involved in the process, the more impactful will be the experience.

Step 3: Study the hymn. There are two objectives at this stage. **The first objective is comprehension.** Do the grunt work of looking up words in a dictionary that you do not know; of thinking about word pictures that may be unexpected or obscure; and of listening for echoes of familiar Bible passages. Keep in mind that learning is the joint child of effort and curiosity. The more willing you are to ask questions of the hymn – and the more diligent you are to find answers to your questions – the more absorbed in the process the mind will become. Insight and retention will be the dividends of such exertion.

The second objective is to use the hymn as a launch point for further exploration of the Scriptures. There is a unique thrill that comes from seeing the unity and coherence of God's Word. In the margin beside each hymn, there will be Scripture passages that are either direct quotations, indirect allusions, or supporting passages. Look these up and spend time reflecting both on how the Scriptures illumine the hymn, and how the hymn illumines the Scriptures.[1]

Step 4: Pray. If these hymns are used for sustained meditation, I can all but promise that, at some point in the exercise, the coals of the heart will catch aflame. When this happens, it is time to put the hymn down and to offer a spiritual sacrifice of worship to God. At the end of the day, if these hymns produce prayer, the exercise is a success. Communion with God: this is the highest achievement of any spiritual exercise.

How long will it take to complete a single workout? This is a difficult question to answer. Twenty minutes should be sufficient for the grunt work to be finished. What happens beyond that is in the hands of the Holy Spirit. William Cowper says, in one of his most famous hymns, 'Sometimes a light surprises the Christian while he sings.' The key word here is *sometimes*. Don't expect each day's work to conclude with a stunning sunset and a fairytale rainbow. Unlike Disney, God doesn't promise

---

1   There is no need to look up every reference in the margin. Allow interest and curiosity to be your guide.

fireworks every day. But, now and again, a special grace will fall like dew on the prayerful heart. These are precious moments to be relished and savored. My prayer is that there will be many such 'trysts' with God for believers who patiently work through the exercises in this book.

Finally, a word should be said about how the particular hymns in this book have been selected. They are not necessarily the very best hymns that have been written, if the criterion being used is artistic sensibility. Neither have they been chosen due to popularity. Almost all of them will be unfamiliar to modern Christians. They have been selected for one reason: the point of view that they provide for spiritual meditation. Each is like a hidden peak that is worth climbing in order to survey the landscape of divine beauty. One by one, they will fling open new horizons of devotion that are every bit as breathtaking and soul refreshing as a solitary perch on the edge of a vast canyon:

Jesus, these eyes have never seen
That radiant form of thine;
The veil of sense hangs dark between
Thy blessed face and mine.

I see thee not, I hear thee not,
Yet art thou oft with me;
And earth hath ne'er so dear a spot
As where I meet with thee.

Outline of Exercises

The Holiness of God
The Mystery of the Gospel
       Incarnation and Life
       Death
       Resurrection and Ascension
       Final Judgment and New Creation
Spiritual Fellowship
       The Father
       The Son
       The Holy Spirit
       The Church
Spiritual Transformation
       Inward Motivation
       Mature Character
Spiritual Disciplines
       Bible Reading
       Prayer
       Repentance and Mortification
Practicing the Presence of God
       Whole-Life Discipleship
Spiritual Trials
       Suffering and Affliction
       Temptation and Spiritual Warfare
       Facing Death

1

Meditating on the Holiness of God

In C. S. Lewis's novel, *Prince Caspian,* there is a scene in which Lucy comments to Aslan, 'You're bigger.' Unexpectedly, he replies, 'That is because you are older, little one.' The response confuses Lucy. She muses, 'Not because you are?' Aslan answers, 'I am not, but every year you grow, you will find me bigger.'[1]

God's holiness is unchanging. However, our appreciation of His holiness ought to be changing all of the time. It is a significant sign of the Spirit at work in our hearts when, suddenly, God looks a little bigger, more majestic, and more praiseworthy than He did before. This growth of awe is an unmistakable sign of the Spirit at work in our hearts. It is no exaggeration to say that the life of heaven will be an ongoing experience of surprise as God, yet again, breaks through whatever ceiling of knowledge we thought could contain the wonder of His being. That said, we do not need to wait until heaven to get a

1   C. S. Lewis, *Prince Caspian* (London: Harpers Collins, 2008).

foretaste of such amazement. The purpose of this first set of hymns is to whet the appetite of worship. Each hymn has an unusual ability to widen the eyes of faith, thereby enabling us to glimpse more of the inexhaustible mystery that angels never tire of beholding.

Now, three facets of divine holiness merit special attention as we move into these hymns. The first is the transcendence of God. Modern Christians routinely reduce God to 'god', a concept that is small, tame, and devoid of mystery. The hymns in this section are a powerful tool to demolish the idols of the mind and, in their place, resurrect a true knowledge of the holy, knowledge which is built on fearful wonder and joyful adoration.

Second, these hymns remind us that, while God's being is infinite, His character is not amorphous. He is not a cloud which refuses to take a definite shape. The contrary is true. We can know God precisely because He has revealed Himself through specific traits like faithfulness, mercy, love, goodness, justice, and wisdom. Most of the hymns in this section focus on a key character trait, or attribute, of God. One benefit of studying these hymns will be clarity regarding two of the most important questions that anyone can ask: 'Who is God?' and, 'Why should I trust Him?'

Finally, these hymns trace an often-overlooked connection between beauty and holiness. Whenever God chooses to reveal His glory, He always creates something that includes color, form, movement, life, sound and love. This was true of the creation of our world. It was also true of the blueprint that God gave Moses for the Tabernacle. A lesson we should learn from this connection is that the perception of beauty and an encounter with holiness are analogous experiences. We can no more stand dis-interested in the presence of the Holy One than we can be indifferent at the scene of an unforgettable sunset. A true comprehension of holiness always results in worship. We know that we have glimpsed the shadow of the Living God when our hearts cry out with the seraphim, 'Holy, holy, holy is the Lord of hosts' (Isa. 6:3).

1 – Divine Transcendence

Reading: Isaiah 6:1-5

Eternal pow'r whose high abode	Isa. 57:15
Becomes[1] the grandeur of a God	
Infinite lengths beyond the bounds	1 Kings 8:27
Where stars revolve their little rounds.[2]	

The lowest step above thy seat,
Rises too high for Gabriel's feet.
In vain the tall arch-angel tries;
To reach the height with wond'ring eyes.

Lord what shall earth and ashes do?	Gen. 2:7, 3:19
We would adore our Maker too;	
From sin and dust to thee we cry	
The great, the holy and the high!	

Earth from afar has heard thy fame,	
And worms have learnt to lisp thy name;	Ps. 22:6, 8:2
But O the glories of thy mind	
Leave all our soaring thoughts behind.	Rom. 11:33

God is in heav'n and men below	Ps. 115:3
Be short our tunes, our words be few!	
A sacred rev'rence checks our songs	
And praise sits silent on our tongues.	Hab. 2:20, Rev. 8:1

ISAAC WATTS

---

1   In the sense of 'is fitting for' or 'suitable for.'

2   If one judges by ordinary perception, not scientific models, the stars appear small and look as if they revolve around the earth.

Reflection Questions:

1. This hymn inspires us to think about how God is 'the great, the holy, and the high.' Think about these three adjectives. What does it mean that God is great, holy, and high?

2. Reread the second stanza. What does it mean that 'The lowest step above thy seat,/Rises too high for Gabriel's feet?' How does this image help us to marvel at the transcendence of God?

3. Why is silence at times the most appropriate expression of worship (c.f. Hab. 2:20; Zeph. 1:7; Zech. 2:13; Rev. 8:1)?

2 – *The Incomprehensibility of God*

Reading: Exodus 24:15-18

God is a name my soul adores,	
Th'Almighty THREE, th'eternal ONE!	
Nature and grace, with all their powers	Rom. 1:20, John 1:14
Confess the infinite unknown.	1 Tim. 6:16
Thy voice produc'd the sea and spheres,	Ps. 33:6-7
Bid the waves roar, and planets shine;	Ps. 29:3
But nothing like thyself appears,	Isa. 40:18
Through all these spacious works of thine.	Deut. 4:15
Still restless nature dies and grows;	Isa. 51:6
From change to change the creatures run;	
Thy being no succession knows,	Ps. 90:1-2
And all thy vast designs are one.	Rom. 11:36
Thrones and dominions round thee fall,	Col. 1:16
And worship in submissive forms;	Rev. 4:10
Thy presence shakes this lower ball,[1]	Heb. 12:25-29
This little dwelling place of worms.	
How shall affrighted mortals dare	Exod. 20:18-21
To sing thy glory or thy grace?	
Beneath thy feet we lie so far,	Exod. 24:10
And see but shadows of thy face!	Exod. 33:20-23
Who can behold this blazing light!	Rev. 1:16
Who can approach consuming flame?	Isa. 33:14
None but thy wisdom knows thy might,	
None but thy word can speak thy name.	John 1:1,18

ISAAC WATTS

---

1   Earth

Reflection Questions:

1. The hymn says that God is 'the infinite unknown.' How is it possible for God both to be truly known and yet infinitely unknown at the same time?

2. According to the second stanza, creation lacks the ability to communicate the identity of God. Why is this?[2]

3. What is the meaning of the final line in the hymn? Who is the 'word' that speaks the name of God (c.f. John 1:1)?

---

2   In another hymn, Watts writes, 'Nature, to make his beauties known,/ Must mingle colors not her own.' See 'Go, Worship at Immanuel's Feet.'

3 – *The Beauty of Holiness*

Reading: Revelation 4:1-11

My God, how wonderful thou art,	
Thy majesty how bright!	Ps. 104:1-2
How beautiful thy mercy seat,	Heb. 9:5, 11
In depths of burning light!	Matt. 17:2, Ps. 36:9
Wondrous are Thine eternal years,	
O everlasting Lord,	Rev. 22:13
By holy angels day and night	
Unceasingly adored!	Isa. 6:1-3
How beautiful, how beautiful,	1 Chron. 16:29
The sight of Thee must be,	
Thine endless wisdom, boundless pow'r,	
And awesome purity!	
O how I fear thee, living God,	
With deepest, tend'rest fears,	Ps. 103:13-14
And worship Thee with trembling hope	
And penitential tears!	Luke 7:37-38
Yet I may love Thee too, O Lord,	
Almighty as thou art,	
For thou hast stooped to ask of me	
The love of my poor heart.	Rom. 8:15
No earthly father loves like thee,	Matt. 7:11
No mother, e'er so mild	Isa. 49:15
Bears and forbears, as Thou hast done	
With me, Thy sinful child.	Luke 15:21
Father of Jesus, Love divine,	John 20:17
What rapture it will be,	
Prostrate before Thy throne to lie,	
And gaze and gaze on Thee!	Matt. 5:8

FREDERICK FABER

Reflection Questions:

1. How would you describe the beauty of God? What does it mean that God is beautiful?

2. How should fear and love combine in the worship of God?

3. What do you think it will be like to gaze on the beauty of God? Can you recall any experiences that provide a faint taste of encountering something unspeakably glorious?

4 – *The Mystery of the Trinity*

Readings: 2 Corinthians 13:14, Matthew 3:16-17

We give immortal praise	
To God the Father's love,	
For all our comforts here,	
And better hopes above;	
He sent His own eternal Son,	John 3:16
To die for sins that man had done.	1 Pet. 3:18
To God the Son belongs	
Immortal glory too,	1 Tim. 1:17
Who bought us with His blood	Acts 20:28, Col. 1:14
From everlasting woe:	
And now He lives, and now He reigns,	Rev. 1:18
And sees the fruit of all His pains.	
To God the Spirit's name	
Immortal worship give,	
Whose new-creating power	Gen. 1:2, 2 Cor. 5:17
Makes the dead sinner live;	John 3:5-8
His work completes the great design,	John 14:16
And fills the soul with joy divine.	John 15:11
Almighty God, to Thee	
Be endless honors done,	
The undivided Three,	Matt. 28:19
And the mysterious One:	Deut. 6:4
Where reason fails, with all her powers,	
There faith prevails, and love adores.	1 Cor. 13:12-13

ISAAC WATTS

Reflection Questions:

1. How do we see all three persons of the Trinity working together in this hymn?

2. What role does each person of the Trinity play in our redemption?

3. What is the meaning of the final two lines of the hymn? What does it mean for faith to prevail where reason fails? What does it mean to adore what we cannot fully understand?

5 – *The Eternity of God*

Readings: Job 38:1-7, Psalm 90:1-2

Great former of this various frame,	Heb. 11:3
Our souls adore Thine awful[1] name;	
And bow and tremble while they praise	
The Ancient of eternal days.	Dan. 7:9-10
Thou, Lord, with unsurprised survey,	Isa. 46:9-10
Saw'st nature rising yesterday;	2 Pet. 3:8
And, as tomorrow, shall Thine eye	
See earth and stars in ruin lie.	Isa. 34:4
Beyond an angel's vision bright,	
Thou dwell'st in self existent light;	1 John 1:5
Which shines, with undiminished ray,	
While suns and worlds in smoke decay.	Ps. 102:25-27
Our days a transient period run,	
And change with every circling sun;	Eccles. 1:3-4
And, in the firmest state we boast,	
A moth can crush us into dust.	Job 4:19
But let the creatures fall around;	
Let death consign us to the ground;	
Let the last general flame arise,	2 Pet. 3:10-12
And melt the arches of the skies:	
Calm as the summer's ocean, we	
Can all the wreck of nature see,	
While grace secures us an abode,	John 14:3
Unshaken as the throne of God.	Heb. 12:27-28

PHILIP DODDRIDGE

---

1   Awful here is used in the old sense of 'awesome' or 'awe-inspiring.'

Reflection Questions:

1. How is our perception of the universe changed when we set the universe beside an eternal and unchanging God? Consider the first three stanzas for food for thought.

2. Ps. 90:12 says, 'Teach us to number our days, that we might gain a heart of wisdom.' What wisdom do we gain from contemplating our finitude and our mortality?

3. The final stanza compares the peace of a believer to the calm of a quiet ocean. What is the source of this astounding peace in the midst of so much change, chaos, and upheaval? See Psalm 46:10 for further insight.

6 – The Omnipotence of God

Reading: Psalm 99:1-5

The Lord is King! Lift up thy voice,
O earth, and all ye heavens, rejoice!
From world to world the joy shall ring,
The Lord Omnipotent[1] is King.   Ps. 95:3

The Lord is King! Who then shall dare
Resist His will, distrust His care,
Or murmur at His wise decrees,
Or doubt His royal promises?   Num. 23:19

The Lord is King! Child of the dust,
The Judge of all the earth is just;   Gen. 18:25
Holy and true are all His ways,   Deut. 32:4
Let every creature speak His praise.

He reigns! Ye saints, exalt your strains;   Rev. 19:6
Your God is King, your Father reigns;
And He is at the Father's side,   Heb. 1:3
The Man of love, the Crucified.

Come, make your wants, your burdens
     known;   Ps. 55:22, 1 Pet. 5:7
He will present them at the throne;
This world of ours and worlds unseen;
How thin the boundary between!

Oh! When His wisdom can mistake,
His might decay, His love forsake,
Then may His children cease to sing,
The Lord Omnipotent is King.

---

1   Omnipotence means all-powerful.

One Lord, one empire, all secures: 1 Cor. 8:6
He reigns – and life and death are yours.   1 Cor. 3:22
Through earth and heaven one song shall ring:
'The Lord Omnipotent is King.'

JOSEPH CONDER

Reflection Questions:

1. Ponder the second stanza. What are some symptoms mentioned that indicate a lapse of belief in the omnipotence of God?

2. Reread the fifth stanza. How is faith in the omnipotence of God a strong motive for prayer? How would your prayers be different today if you were trusting more fully in the omnipotence of God?

3. Explain the logic of the second-to-last stanza. What point is being made in these lines? How is this point reiterated in final lines of the hymn?

7 – *The Omnipresence and Omniscience of God*[1]

Reading: Psalm 139:1-6

In all my vast concerns with Thee,
In vain my soul would try
To shun Thy presence, Lord, or flee
The notice of Thine eye.

Thy all-surrounding sight surveys
My rising and my rest,   Ps. 139:2
My public walks, my private ways,
And secrets of my breast.   Ps. 44:21

My thoughts lie open to the Lord   Heb. 4:13
Before they're formed within;
And ere my lips pronounce the word
He knows the sense I mean.   Ps. 139:4

O wondrous knowledge, deep and high!
Where can a creature hide?   Ps. 139:7
Within Thy circling arms I lie,
Beset on every side.   Deut. 33:12, 27

So let Thy grace surround me still,   Ps. 125:2
And like a bulwark prove,   Isa. 26:1
To guard my soul from every ill,
Secured by sovereign love.

Lord, where shall guilty souls retire,
Forgotten and unknown?
In hell they meet Thy dreadful fire,
In Heav'n Thy glorious throne.   Ps. 139:8

---

1 Omnipresence means being present everywhere, and omniscience means knowing everything.

Should I suppress my vital breath
To 'scape the wrath divine,
Thy voice would break the bars of death,
And make the grave resign.[2]   Rev. 20:13

If winged with beams of morning light
I fly beyond the west,
Thy hand, which must support my flight,
Would soon betray my rest.   Ps. 139:9

If o'er my sins I think to draw
The curtains of the night,
Those flaming eyes that guard Thy law   Rev. 1:14, 19:12
Would turn the shades to light.   Ps. 139:11-12

The beams of noon, the midnight hour,
Are both alike to Thee: Dan. 2:22
O may I ne'er provoke that power
From which I cannot flee.   Ps. 139:23-24

Isaac Watts

Reflection Questions:

1. How is the omniscience of God a source of comfort for Christians?

2. How is the omniscience of God a source of godly fear for Christians?

3. Reread the last two stanzas. Why do we sometimes willfully ignore the omniscience of God?

---

2   The grave cannot hide us from God.

8 – *The Faithfulness of God*

Reading: Psalm 36:5-10

Praise, everlasting praise, be paid	
To him that earth's foundation laid;	Ps. 104:5
Praise to the God whose strong decrees	Ps. 33:9
Sway the creation as he please.	Ps. 115:3

Praise to the goodness of the Lord,	
Who rules his people by his word,	Ps. 33:10-11
And there, as strong as his decrees,	
He sets his kindest promises.	

Firm are the words his prophets give,	Num. 23:19
Sweet words on which his children live;	Matt. 4:4
Each of them is the voice of God,	
Who spoke, and spread the skies abroad.	Gen. 1:6

Each of them powerful as that sound	Ps. 29:5
That bid the new-made world go round;	Gen. 1
And stronger than the solid poles	
On which the wheel of nature rolls.	

Whence then should doubts and fears arise?
Why trickling sorrows drown our eyes?
Slowly, alas! our mind receives
The comfort that our Maker gives.

O for a strong, a lasting faith,	
To credit what th' Almighty saith!	Rom. 4:3
T' embrace the message of his Son,	
And call the joys of heav'n our own.	

Then should the earth's old pillars shake,	1 Sam. 2:8
And all the wheels of nature break,	Ps. 46:2-3
Our steady souls should fear no more	
Than solid rocks when billows roar.	Ps. 62:2

Our everlasting hopes arise
Above the ruinable skies,   Heb. 1:10-12
Where the eternal Builder reigns,   Heb. 3:4
And his own courts his power sustains.[1]

ISAAC WATTS

Reflection Questions:

1. What is the difference between a 'decree' and a 'promise'? Why is it important to know that the promises of God are as firm and fixed as the decrees of God?

2. The hymn claims that our faith can be as strong as 'solid rocks' in the midst of billowing waves. What is the source of such faith?

3. The great missionary, Hudson Taylor, once said that Christians do not need great faith, but faith in a great God. How does the hymn communicate this same truth?

---

1   Isaac Watts has another wonderful hymn, very similar to this one, 'Begin, My Soul, Some Heav'nly Theme.'

9 – *The Love of God*

Reading: Psalm 136:1-9

Thy ceaseless, unexhausted love,	
Unmerited and free,	
Delights our evil to remove,	Micah 7:18
And help our misery.	
Thou waitest to be gracious still;	Isa. 30:18
Thou dost with sinners bear,	Rom. 2:4
That, saved, we may thy goodness feel,	
And all thy grace declare.	Ps. 51:14-15
Thy goodness and thy truth to me,	Ps. 23:6
To ev'ry soul abound,	
A vast, unfathomable sea,	
Where all our thoughts are drowned.	
Its streams the whole creation reach,	Ps. 65:9
So plenteous is the store,	
Enough for all, enough for each,	
Enough for evermore.	
Faithful, O Lord, thy mercies are,	
A rock that cannot move;	Ps. 18:2
A thousand promises declare	
Thy constancy of love.	1 Chron. 16:34
Throughout the universe it reigns,	Rom. 5:21
Unalterably sure;	
And while the truth of God remains	
The goodness must endure.	Ps. 100:5

CHARLES WESLEY

Reflection Questions:

1. The hymn begins by stating that God's love is 'ceaseless', 'unexhausted', 'unmerited', and 'free'. Take a moment to reflect on each of these words. Which word is of greatest comfort to you?

2. The hymn uses three images to explore the love of God: a sea, a stream, and a rock. How does each image reveal something unique and special about the love of God?

3. Reflect on the final two lines of the hymn. How are the truth of God and the goodness of God like the two wings of an airplane, each working together to support the faith of a believer?

10 – The Majesty of God

Reading: Psalm 104:1-9

We sing th' almighty pow'r of God,
Who bade the mountains rise,
Who spread the flowing seas abroad
And built the lofty skies.   Gen. 1:1-10

We sing the wisdom that ordain'd
The sun to rule the day;
The moon shines full at his command,
And all the stars obey.   Gen. 1:14-19

We sing the goodness of the Lord,
Who fills the earth with food;
Who form'd the creatures by a word
And then pronounc'd them good.   Gen. 1:11-13

Lord, how your wonders are display'd,
Where'er we turn our eyes;
Whether we view the ground we tread
Or gaze upon the skies!   Ps. 19:1-4

There's not a plant nor flow'r below,
But makes your glories known;   Ps. 104:24
And clouds arise and tempests blow,
By order from thy throne.   Ps. 135:7

Creation, vast as it may be,
Is subject to thy will.   Ps. 119:91
There's not a place, where we can flee,
But God is with us still.   Jer. 23:24

In heaven He shines with beams of love,
With wrath in hell beneath;
'Tis on His earth I stand or move,
And 'tis His air I breathe.   Acts 17:24-25

His hand is my perpetual guard,
He guides me with His eye: Ps. 32:8
Why should I then forget the Lord,
Who is forever nigh?[1]

ISAAC WATTS

Reflection Questions:

1. The first line of each of the first three stanzas picks up on a different attribute of God – power, wisdom, and goodness. How does God's creation reveal each one of these?

2. The hymn says that 'There is not a plant or flow'r below/But makes your glories known.' What can we learn about the glory of God from observing simple things like grass and flowers?

3. One of the great dangers of the Christian life is losing sight of the presence of God. How can celebrating the glory of God as revealed in creation help us to be more aware of the presence of God?

---

1   Another classic hymn that captures something of the majesty of God is 'Immortal, Invisible, God Only Wise' by Walter Smith. It is included as a later exercise in this book.

2

MEDITATING ON THE MYSTERY OF THE GOSPEL

The great apologist, G. K. Chesterton, once wrote, 'The next best thing to being really inside of Christendom is to be really outside of it.'[1] His point was that, in the process of a culture gradually losing its Christian moorings, we often take for granted the startling and wonderful truths of the gospel. The drama of our doctrines is flattened out into a set of beliefs that no longer titillate the mind or ravish the heart. If there is anyone on the verge of being able to recite the Apostles Creed without a rush of adrenalin revving his heart, the hymns in this section are for you. They are like silver polish for a set of flatware that has lost its shine. The mind that earnestly grapples with them will discover a joyful, sparkling light dancing on old, familiar truths.

Now, there are three main objectives to keep in view while studying these hymns. The first objective is to fill in important gaps of understanding and belief. A lot of

---

1   G. K. Chesterton, *The Everlasting Man,* introduction.

Christians, for example, spend very little time reflecting on the importance of Christ's ascension and His high priestly ministry. We have a clear sense of what Jesus was doing on earth; however, we're not quite sure what He's up to now that He's in heaven. The arrangement of these hymns is intended to stretch the boundaries of thought so that unexplored pastures of the gospel are unlocked and explored.

A second objective is to find new vistas from which to observe old truths. It is one thing to visit the Grand Canyon and observe it from one of the central tourist hubs; it is something else to climb down into the Canyon and view its ridges and walls from within. The Canyon itself does not change if we view it from the top or from the bottom. However, viewing the canyon from a different angle will yield a different perspective. The beauty of the Canyon will be encountered in novel ways if we are willing to move about and change our location.

These hymns have a special power to shift the point of view from which we look at core elements of the gospel. The hymns included on the subject of the cross of Christ bear exceptional witness to this power. As many have noted, the cross is like a diamond. No single angle can reveal the full landscape of its meaning. Thus, studying multiple hymns on the cross is like standing and observing the death of Christ from a number of different perspectives. Each hymn will bring into focus a unique and awe-inspiring vista of what Christ has accomplished through His work at Calvary.

A third objective for studying these hymns is worship. These hymns are food for both the heart and the mind. Each of them was conceived by a worshipping heart, and, if used for prolonged and patient prayer, they will continue to generate spiritual life among those who meditate on them. Read them as scripts for devotion. Do not just put on their thoughts; get dressed in their passions. Rehearse them again and again in the mind until their spirit becomes your spirit. Peter's exhortation ought to be remembered as we dedicate time to reflect on these hymns: 'Like newborn infants, long for pure spiritual milk, that by it you may grow up into salvation – if indeed you have tasted that the Lord is good' (1 Pet. 2:2-3). I can guarantee one thing about the following hymns: they are pure spiritual milk.

11 – *The Eternal Love of the Father*

Reading: Ephesians 1:1-14

'Twas not to make Jehovah's love	
Towards the sinner flame,	
That Jesus, from His throne above,	
A suffering man became.	John 3:16

'Twas not the death which He endured,	
Nor all the pang He bore,	
That God's eternal love procured,	Eph. 1:4
For God was love before.	1 John 4:16

He loved the world of His elect	
With love surpassing thought;	Eph. 3:19
Nor will His mercy e'er neglect	
The souls so dearly bought.	Rom. 8:31-2

The warm affections of His breast	
Towards His chosen burn;	Jer. 31:3
And in His love He'll ever rest,	
Nor from His oath return.	Isa. 45:23

Still to confirm His oath of old,	
See in the heavens His bow;	Gen. 9:13
No fierce rebukes, but love untold	
Awaits His children now.	Rom. 5:5

JOHN KENT

Reflection Questions:

1. Some Christians wrongly think that Jesus had to die in order to convince the Father to love us. How does this hymn correct this dangerous misconception?

2. What do we learn about our heavenly Father from the hymn? Pay attention to the details of the hymn.

3. How are the final two lines of the hymn an encouragement to prayer?

12 – *The Eternal Love of the Son*

Reading: Proverbs 8:22-31

Ere God had built the mountains,	Prov. 8:25
Or raised the fruitful hills;	
Before He filled the fountains	Prov. 8:24
That feed the running rills;	
In me from everlasting,	Prov. 8:22-23
The wonderful I Am,	
Found pleasures never wasting,	Prov. 8:30
And Wisdom is my name.	Prov. 8:1, I Cor. 1:24
When, like a tent to dwell in,	Isa. 40:22
He spread the skies abroad,	
And swathed about the swelling	
Of Ocean's mighty flood;	Prov. 8:29
He wrought by weight and measure,	
And I was with Him then:	Prov. 8:30, John 1:1-5
Myself the Father's pleasure,	Matt. 3:17, 17:5
And mine, the sons of men.	Prov. 8:31
Thus Wisdom's words discover	
Thy glory and Thy grace,	John 1:14
Thou everlasting Lover	Jer. 31:3
Of our unworthy race!	
Thy gracious eye surveyed us	
Ere stars were seen above;	Eph. 1:4
In wisdom Thou hast made us,	Ps. 104:24
And died for us in love.	1 John 3:16

And couldst Thou be delighted
With creatures such as we,
Who, when we saw Thee, slighted,
And nailed Thee to a tree?
Unfathomable wonder,
And mystery divine!   Eph. 3:4
The voice that speaks in thunder,   Ps. 29:3
Says, Sinner, I am thine!

WILLIAM COWPER

Reflection Questions:

1. Christians have traditionally understood the personified wisdom of Proverbs 8 to be a description of Christ. How does the hymn help us to make this connection between wisdom and Christ?

2. With all of the universe at His feet, why does God have a special love for human beings?

3. The final stanza is meant to generate feelings of surprise, shock, and wonder. What is your emotional response to the final lines of the hymn?

13 – The Glory of God Incarnate

Reading: Colossians 1:15-20

Hark! the Herald, Angels sing,	Luke 2:13-14
"Glory to the new born King;	
Peace on Earth, and Mercy mild,	
God and Sinners reconciled."	Rom. 5:10
Joyful all ye Nations rise,	
Join the Triumphs of the Skies,	
With th' angelic Host proclaim,	
Christ is born in Bethlehem.	Luke 2:11
Christ by highest Heaven ador'd,	Phil. 2:9-10
Christ the everlasting Lord;	
Late in Time behold him come,	Gal. 4:4
Offspring of a Virgin's Womb;	Isa. 7:14, Matt. 1:23-25
Veil'd in Flesh, the Godhead see,	Col. 1:19, Heb. 1:3
Hail th' Incarnate Deity!	John 1:14
Pleas'd as Man with men t' appear,	Phil. 2:7-8
Jesus, our Immanuel here.	Isa. 7:14
Hail the Heav'n born Prince of Peace!	Isa. 9:6
Hail, the Son of Righteousness!	Mal. 4:2
Light and Life to all he brings,	John 1:4
Ris'n with Healing in his Wings;	Mal. 4:2
Mild he lays his Glory by,	Phil. 2:5-7
Born, that Man no more may die,	Heb. 2:14
Born to raise the sons of Earth;	Rom. 8:21-23
Born to give them second Birth.	John 3:7

Come, Desire of Nations, come,	Hag. 2:7
Fix in us thy humble Home;	Isa. 57:15
Rise, the Woman's conq'ring seed,	Gen. 3:15, Rev. 12:13
Bruise in us the Serpent's Head;	Rom. 16:20
Adam's Likeness now efface,	
Stamp thine Image in its Place;	1 Cor. 15:49
Second Adam from above,	1 Cor. 15:45-47
Re-instate us in thy Love.[1]	

CHARLES WESLEY

Reflection Questions:

1. Reflect on the line 'Veil'd in Flesh, the Godhead see.' How should this truth affect how we read the gospel stories? What difference does it make to recognize that Jesus is God-in-flesh?

2. C. S. Lewis famously said, 'The central miracle asserted by Christians is the incarnation.'[2] Why is the miracle of God becoming man an essential part of the gospel?

3. The coming of Christ is the fulfilment of numerous Old Testament promises and prophecies. How does the hymn demonstrate the way in which the birth of Jesus is the fulfilment of God's Word?

---

1 Another unforgettable hymn on the beauty of God revealed through the incarnation is 'God Worship at Immanuel's Feet' by Isaac Watts. Be sure to read the original hymn which has eighteen stanzas.

2 See C. S. Lewis, *Miracles*, chapter 14.

14 – *The Incarnation Transforms Our Knowledge of God*

Reading: John 1:14-18

Dearest of all the names above,	Phil. 2:10
My Jesus, and my God,	John 20:28
Who can resist Thy heavenly love,	Ps. 63:3
Or trifle with Thy blood?	Heb. 10:29
'Tis by the merits of Thy death	
The Father smiles again;	Rom. 5:8-10
'Tis by Thine interceding breath	
The Spirit dwells with men.	John 14:16
Till God in human flesh I see,	John 1:14
My thoughts no comfort find;	
The holy, just, and sacred Three	
Are terrors to my mind.	Rom. 1:18
But if Immanuel's face appear,	Rom. 3:21-22
My hope, my joy begins;	
His name forbids my slavish fear,	Rom. 8:15, 1 John 4:18
His grace removes my sins.	Rom. 3:23-24
While Jews on their own law rely,	
And Greeks of wisdom boast,	1 Cor. 1:23
I love th'incarnate mystery,	
And there I fix my trust.	1 Cor. 1:30

ISAAC WATTS

Reflection Questions:

1. Think about the third stanza. Why is our knowledge of God a source of fear, not comfort, if we think about God apart from the person and work of Jesus?

2. Reflect on the fourth stanza. How does the face of Jesus, Immanuel, enable slavish fear to be replaced by joy?

3. The final stanza claims that there are only three ways to attempt to know God: through the Old Testament law, through mere human wisdom, and through Jesus. What unique truth does Jesus reveal?

15 – Christ: the Pattern of Perfection

Reading: Luke 4:1-13

My dear Redeemer and my Lord,	
I read my Duty in thy Word;	
But in thy Life the Law appears,	
Drawn out in living Characters.	John 1:14
Such was thy Truth, and such thy Zeal,	John 2:17
Such Def'rence to thy Father's Will,	John 4:34
Such Love, and Meekness so divine,	Luke 23:34
I would transcribe and make them mine.	2 Cor. 3:3
Cold Mountains, and the Midnight Air	Mark 1:35
Witness'd the Fervour of thy Pray'r;	
The Desert thy Temptations knew,	Luke 4:1-13
Thy Conflict, and thy Vict'ry too.	
Be thou my Pattern; make me bear	Eph. 4:20
More of thy gracious Image here;	Col. 3:10
Then God, the Judge, shall own my Name	
Amongst the Foll'wers of the Lamb.	Rev. 7:14

Isaac Watts

Reflection Questions:

1. Imitating Christ is a difficult topic. What aspects of the life of Christ are we called to imitate? What aspects of His life are unique and unrepeatable?

2. What specific traits or actions of Christ does this hymn suggest that we ought to 'transcribe' and 'make [our] own?'

3. The ending of this hymn might confuse some readers. A careless reading might lead one to think that the hymn is saying that God accepts us due to our performance. Yet, Isaac Watts, the hymn-writer, had a profound understanding of grace. What evidence is there in the hymn to guard us from this misunderstanding? (Hint: don't forget the first line!)

16 – *The Miracles of Grace*

Reading: John 5:1-15

Jesus, if still thou art to-day	
As yesterday the same,	Heb. 13:8
Present to heal, in me display	
The virtue of thy name.	
If still thou go'st about to do	
Thy needy creatures good,	Ps. 145:9
On me, that I thy praise may show,	Ps. 51:15, Isa. 43:21
Be all thy wonders shew'd.	
Now, Lord, to whom for help I call,	
Thy miracles repeat;	
With pitying eyes behold me fall	
A leper at thy feet.	Matt. 8:1-4
Loathsome, and foul, and self-abhorr'd,	
I sink beneath my sin;	
But if thou wilt, a gracious word	
Of thine can make me clean.	Matt. 8:2
Thou seest me deaf to thy commands,	Mark 7:31-37
Open, O Lord, my ear;	
Bid me stretch out my wither'd hands,	Mark 3:1-6
And lift them up in pray'r.	Ps. 63:4
Silent (alas! thou know'st how long)	
My voice, I cannot raise;	
But O! when thou shalt loose my tongue,	
The dumb shall sing thy praise.	Isa. 35:6
Lame at the pool I still am found:	John 5:8
Give, and my strength employ;	
Light as a hart I then shall bound,	
The lame shall leap for joy.	Isa. 35:6

Blind from my birth to guilt and thee.   John 9
And dark I am within;   Matt. 6:23
The love of God I cannot see,
The sinfulness of sin.

But thou, they say, art passing by,   Mark 10:46-52
O let me find thee near;
Jesus, in mercy, hear my cry,
Thou Son of David, hear.   Mark 10:48

Long have I waited in the way
For thee the heav'nly light;   John 8:12
Command me to be brought, and say,
Sinner, receive thy sight.   Luke 18:42

CHARLES WESLEY

Reflection Questions:

1. How does the first stanza set up the rest of the hymn?

2. The hymn takes a number of different miracles of Christ and reworks them as private prayers. How does the hymn change the meaning of blindness, deafness, and lameness in order to make these conditions relevant to us?

3. How can this hymn help you spend time in confession before Jesus?

17 – The Cross Reveals the Awfulness of Sin

Reading: Isaiah 53:1-12

Stricken, smitten, and afflicted,	Isa. 53:4
See him dying on the tree!	
'Tis the Christ by man rejected;	Isa. 53:2
Yes, my soul, 'tis he, 'tis he!	
'Tis the long-expected Prophet,	
David's Son, yet David's Lord;	Ps. 110:1, Matt. 22:43
By his Son God now has spoken:	
'Tis the true and faithful Word.	Heb. 1:3
Tell me, ye who hear him groaning,	
Was there ever grief like his?	Lam. 1:12
Friends thro' fear his cause disowning,	
Foes insulting his distress;	Mark 15:29
Many hands were raised to wound him,	Zech. 13:6
None would interpose to save;	
But the deepest stroke that pierced him	
Was the stroke that Justice gave.	Isa. 53:10
Ye who think of sin but lightly	
Nor suppose the evil great	
Here may view its nature rightly,	
Here its guilt may estimate.	
Mark the sacrifice appointed,	
See who bears the awful load;	Lev. 16:22
'Tis the Word, the Lord's Anointed,	
Son of Man and Son of God.	

Here we have a firm foundation,	Isa. 28:16
Here the refuge of the lost;	
Christ's the Rock of our salvation,	Ps. 62:6
His the name of which we boast.	Ps. 44:8
Lamb of God, for sinners wounded,	John 1:29
Sacrifice to cancel guilt!	
None shall ever be confounded	1 Pet. 2:6
Who on him their hope have built.[1]	

THOMAS KELLY

Reflection Questions:

1. The hymn says, 'The deepest stroke that pierced him/Was the stroke that Justice gave.' How was the spiritual suffering of Christ on the cross even more painful for Him than the physical suffering that He endured?

2. Look at the third stanza of the hymn. How does the cross help us to measure the evil of sin?

3. How would you describe the experience of meditating on the cross from the perspective of this hymn?

---

1 Two other hymns that are worth meditating on that are similar to this one are 'O Sacred Head Now Wounded' and 'Ah Holy Jesus.' Both have solemn traditional tunes that helpfully communicate the message of each hymn.

18 – *The Power of the Cross to Change Us*

Reading: John 19:17-42

When I survey the wond'rous Cross
On which the Prince of Glory dy'd, Heb. 2:10
My richest Gain I count but Loss, Phil. 3:7-8
And pour Contempt on all my Pride.

Forbid it, Lord, that I should boast, Gal. 6:14
Save in the Death of Christ my God:
All the vain Things that charm me most,
I sacrifice them to his Blood.

See from his Head, his Hands, his Feet,
Sorrow and Love flow mingled down!
Did e'er such Love and Sorrow meet? Isa. 53:3
Or Thorns compose so rich a Crown?

His dying Crimson, like a Robe,
Spreads o'er his Body on the Tree;
Then am I dead to all the Globe, Gal. 6:14
And all the Globe is dead to me.

Were the whole Realm of Nature mine,
That were a Present far too small;
Love so amazing, so divine, Rom. 5:8, John15:13
Demands my Soul, my Life, my All. Luke 14:26

Isaac Watts

Reflection Questions:

1. What does it mean to survey the cross? How is the act of 'surveying' different from taking a casual glance?

2. Pride is at the root of all sin. The first stanza suggests that the cross is a unique means of subduing pride. How does this happen? How does the cross humble the otherwise indomitable ego?

3. The final two stanzas talk about the way in which the cross can redirect our worship. How can gazing upon Jesus on the cross liberate us up from deeply-embedded idols of the heart?

19 – Tarrying beside the Cross

Reading: Psalm 22:1-21

O come and mourn with me awhile;
And tarry here the cross beside;   John 19:25
O come, together let us mourn;
Jesus, our Lord, is crucified.

Have we no tears to shed for Him,
While soldiers scoff and foes deride?
Ah! look how patiently He hangs;
Jesus, our Lord, is crucified.

How fast His hands and feet are nailed;   Ps. 22:16
His blessed tongue with thirst is tied,   John 19:28
His failing eyes are blind with blood:
Jesus, our Lord, is crucified.

Seven times He spoke, seven words of love;
And all three hours His silence cried
For mercy on the souls of men;
Jesus, our Lord, is crucified.

Come, let us stand beneath the cross;
So may the blood from out His side
Fall gently on us drop by drop;   John 19:34
Jesus, our Lord, is crucified.

O break, O break, hard heart of mine!
Thy weak self-love and guilty pride
His Pilate and His Judas were:
Jesus, our Lord, is crucified.

A broken heart, a fount of tears,   Ps. 51:17
Ask, and they will not be denied;
A broken heart love's cradle is:
Jesus, our Lord is crucified.

O love of God! O sin of man!
In this dread act Your strength is tried;
And victory remains with love;   John 19:30
For Thou our Lord, art crucified!

FREDERICK FABER

Reflection Questions:

1. The sixth stanza compares self-love to Pilate and pride to Judas. How is our self-love like Pilate? How is our pride like Judas?

2. The hymn says that 'a broken heart love's cradle is'. Explain the meaning of this statement.

3. Explain the final stanza of the hymn? How was the cross a contest between the sin of man and the love of God?

20 – The Cross as a Personal Encounter

Reading: Acts 9:1-9

In evil long I took delight,
Unawed by shame or fear,
Till a new object struck my sight,
And stopped my wild career.

I saw One hanging on a tree,
In agony and blood,
Who fixed His languid eyes on me,
As near His cross I stood.

Sure, never to my latest breath,
Can I forget that look;
It seemed to charge me with His death,
Though not a word He spoke.   Isa. 53:7, Matt. 26:63

My conscience felt and owned the guilt,
And plunged me in despair,
I saw my sins His blood had spilt,
And helped to nail Him there.

Alas! I knew not what I did,
But now my tears are vain;
Where shall my trembling soul be hid?
For I the Lord have slain.   Acts 2:23

A second look He gave, which said,
I freely all forgive;
This blood is for thy ransom paid;   Mark 10:45
I die that thou mayst live.

Thus, while His death my sin displays
In all its blackest hue,
Such is the mystery of grace,
It seals my pardon too.   Col. 2:13-14

With pleasing grief and mournful joy,
My spirit now is filled;
That I should such a life destroy,
Yet live by Him I killed.[1]

JOHN NEWTON

Reflection Questions:

1. This hymn dramatizes two different modes of encountering Jesus on the cross. What is the effect of the first encounter (stanzas 1-5)?

2. What is the effect of the second encounter (stanzas 6-7)?

3. The hymn ends with the reader filled with 'pleasing grief' and 'mournful joy.' These emotions sound paradoxical. Explain them. How can grief be 'pleasing' and joy 'mournful'?

---

1   Another hymn that captures many of these same themes is 'I see the crowd in Pilate's hall' by Horatius Bonar.

21 – The Cross Is Always Before Us

Reading: I Corinthians 1:18-31

Never further than thy cross,	
Never higher than thy feet!	Luke 7:38
Here earth's precious things seem dross,	Phil. 3:8
Here earth's bitter things grow sweet.	
Gazing thus, our sin we see,	
Learn thy love while gazing thus--	
Sin, which laid the cross on thee,	2 Cor. 5:21
Love which bore the cross for us.	Rom. 5:8
Here we learn to serve and give,	Phil. 2:5
And, rejoicing, self-deny;	Luke 9:23
Here we gather love to live,	
Here we gather faith to die.	
Symbols of our liberty	Gal. 5:1
And our service here unite;	1 Cor. 6:20
Captives, by thy cross set free,	Isa. 61:1
Soldiers of thy cross, we fight.	2 Tim. 2:4
Pressing onward as we can,	Phil. 3:12
Still to this our hearts must tend,	
Where our earliest hopes began,	
There our last aspirings end.	
Till amid the hosts of heaven,	
We, in thee redeemed, complete,	
Through thy cross all sins forgiven,	
Cast our crowns before thy feet.	Rev. 4:10

ELIZABETH CHARLES

Reflection Questions:

1. Explain the first two lines of the hymn. What point are they making?

2. The power of the cross for Christian living is not limited to the forgiveness of sins. How does this hymn broaden our understanding of the power of the cross? What does the cross do for us, besides providing an atonement for sin?[1]

3. Look at the second line of the hymn and the last line of the hymn. Why does the hymn begin and end at the feet of Jesus?

---

1 A similar hymn that lists a variety of benefits of the cross is 'We Sing the Praise of Him Who Died' by Thomas Kelly. It offers a useful point of comparison with this hymn.

22 – *The Cross as a Source of Revelation*

Reading: Revelation 5:1-7

Nature with open volume stands
To spread her Maker's praise abroad,   Ps. 19:1-4
And every labor of his hands
Shows something worthy of our God.   Rom. 1:20

But in the grace that rescued man
His brightest form of glory shines;   John 17:1
Here on the cross 'tis fairest drawn
In precious blood and crimson lines.

Here his whole name appears complete;   Heb. 1:4
Nor wit can guess, nor reason prove
Which of the letters best is writ,
The power, the wisdom, or the love.

O the sweet wonders of that cross
Where God the Savior loved and died;
Her noblest life my spirit draws
From his dear wounds and bleeding side.

I would forever speak his name
In sounds to mortal ears unknown,
With angels join to praise the Lamb,   Rev. 5:6
And worship at his Father's throne.

Isaac Watts

Reflection Questions:

1. How is the cross a unique means of revelation? What does the cross reveal about God that we cannot glean from any other source?

2. What does it mean that God's 'whole name appears complete' at the cross? In what sense was the name of God incomplete in the Old Testament?

3. The hymn speaks of the power, wisdom, and love of God being displayed in the cross. How does the cross reveal each of these divine attributes?

23 – The Resurrection: Christ's Victory over Death

Reading: Matthew 28:1-10

Hosanna to the Prince of Light,	John 8:12
That clothed himself in Clay,	Heb. 2:14
Enter'd the Iron Gates of Death,	
And tore the Bars away.	
Death is no more the King of Dread,	Heb. 2:15
Since our Immanuel rose;	
He took the Tyrant's Sting away,	1 Cor. 15:55
And spoil'd our hellish Foes.	Col. 2:15
See how the Conqu'ror mounts aloft,	
And to his Father flies,	John 20:17
With scars of honor in his Flesh,	John 20:25
And Triumph in his Eyes.	
There our exalted Saviour reigns,	
And scatters Blessings down;	Eph. 4:8
Our Jesus fills the middle seat	
Of the Celestial Throne.	Rev. 5:6
Raise your Devotion, mortal Tongues,	
To reach his blest Abode,	
Sweet be the Accents of your Songs	
To our incarnate God.	John 1:14
Bright Angels, strike your loudest Strings,	Rev. 5:11
Your sweetest Voices raise;	
Let Heav'n and all created Things	
Sound our Immanuel's Praise.[1]	

Isaac Watts

---

1 For a hymn that reveals the broader implications of the resurrection for the wider creation, see 'Awake, Glad Soul, Awake! Awake!' by John Monsell. The hymn uses the imagery of the spring time to remind us that, ultimately, the whole of creation will be resurrected.

Reflection Questions:

1. Christians need to view the resurrection as a triumph over evil. How is this victory pictured in the first three stanzas? Look for key descriptive words.

2. How does the fourth stanza remind us that Jesus is still actively involved in the life of His people?

3. The last two stanzas picture first earth, then heaven, joined in harmony to praise the resurrected king. How does this hymn encourage us to join this choir of joy?

24 – Living a Resurrected Life

Reading: Colossians 3:1-17

Ye faithful souls, who Jesus know,	
If risen indeed with him ye are,	Col. 3:1
Superior to the joys below,	
His resurrection's power declare.	

Your faith by holy tempers prove,	Col. 3:5, 12
By actions show your sins forgiven,	
And seek the glorious things above,	Col. 3:1
And follow Christ, your Head, to heaven.	Heb. 3:1

There your exalted Saviour see,	
Seated at God's right hand again,	Heb. 12:2
In all his Father's majesty,	
In everlasting pomp to reign.	

To him continually aspire,	Phil. 3:11-14
Contending for your native place;	Jude 3
And emulate the angel-choir,	
And only live to love and praise.	

For who by faith your Lord receive,	
Ye nothing seek or want beside;	
Dead to the world and sin ye live,	Col. 3:3
Your creature-love is crucified.	Gal. 2:20

Your real life, with Christ concealed,	Col. 3:3-4
Deep in the Father's bosom lies;	
And, glorious as your Head revealed,	1 John 3:2
Ye soon shall meet him in the skies.	1 Thess. 4:17

CHARLES WESLEY

Reflection Questions:

1. This hymn calls us not only to believe in the resurrection, but to live resurrected lives. Look at the second stanza. How can we 'prove' the truth of the resurrection through our attitudes ('tempers') and actions?

2. The fourth stanza challenges us to contend 'for our native place.' What do you think this means? What is 'our native place' (c.f. Phil. 3:20)?

3. Colossians 3:3 says, 'Your life is hidden with Christ in God.' How does this hymn help us – not only to understand – but to live according to this truth?

25 – *The Glory of the Ascended King*

Reading: Revelation 1:9-20

O the Delights, the heav'nly Joys,
The Glories of the Place,
Where Jesus sheds the brightest Beams
Of his o'erflowing Grace!   Rev. 1:16

Sweet Majesty and awful[1] Love
Sit smiling on his Brow,   Rev. 1:17
And all the glorious Ranks above,
At humble Distance bow.   Rev. 5:8

Princes to his imperial Name,
Bend their bright Sceptres down,
Dominions, Thrones, and Pow'rs rejoice   Col. 1:16
To see him wear the Crown.

Archangels sound his lofty Praise
Through ev'ry heav'nly Street;
And lay their highest Honours down,
Submissive at his Feet.   Rev. 4:10

Those soft, those blessed Feet of his,
That once rude Iron tore,
High on a Throne of Light they stand,
And all the Saints adore.

His Head, the dear Majestic Head,
That cruel Thorns did wound,
See what immortal Glories shine,
And circle it around.

---

1   Awful' here means worthy of awe or awe-inspiring.

This is the Man, th' exalted Man,
Whom we unseen adore;   1 Pet. 1:8
But when our Eyes behold his Face,
Our Hearts shall love him more.   1 John 3:2

Lord, how our Souls are all on Fire
To see thy blest Abode,
Our Tongues rejoice in Tunes of Praise
To our incarnate God.

And whilst our Faith enjoys this Sight, 2 Cor. 4:6
We long to leave our Clay,   Phil. 1:21
And wish thy fiery Chariots, Lord, 2 Kings 2:11
To fetch our Souls away.

ISAAC WATTS

Reflection Questions:

1. As Christians, we need to be able, not only to imagine the suffering of Christ on the cross, but also the glory of Christ as revealed in the resurrection and ascension. How does this hymn provide a window into heaven?

2. The second stanza describes the face of Jesus as reflecting 'sweet majesty' and 'awful [awe-inspiring] love.' What do you think it would be like to see Jesus in His glorified condition?

3. During Jesus' death, a crown of thorns scarred His brow and nails pierced His feet. According to the hymn, what happens to the feet and head of Jesus once He is installed as king of heaven?

26 – The High Priestly Ministry of Christ

Reading: Hebrews 7:20–8:2

Before the throne of God above,	Heb. 1:3
I have a strong and perfect plea,	
A great High Priest whose name is Love,	Heb. 4:14
Who ever lives and pleads for me.	Heb. 7:24
My name is graven on his hands,	
My name is written on his heart.	Exod. 28:21
I know that while in heav'n he stands	Heb. 8:1
No tongue can bid me thence depart,	Rom. 8:34
When Satan tempts me to despair	Rev. 12:10
And tells me of the guilt within,	
Upward I look, and see him there,	
Who made an end to all my sin.	Heb. 10:10
Because the sinless Savior died,	Heb. 4:15
My sinful soul is counted free;	
For God, the just, is satisfied	Rom. 3:26
To look on him and pardon me,	1 Pet. 3:18
Behold him there, the risen Lamb,	John 1:29
My perfect, spotless righteousness,	1 Pet. 1:19
The great unchangeable I AM,	John 8:58
The King of glory and of grace!	Ps. 24:7
One with himself I cannot die.	Gal. 2:20
My soul is purchased by his blood!	1 Pet. 1:19
My life is hid with Christ on high,	Col. 3:4
With Christ, my Savior and my God.	

CHARITIE LEES BANCROFT

Reflection Questions:

1. How does this hymn help us to understand the nature of Jesus' high priestly ministry?

2. Why is the thought of our names being written on Jesus' hands and heart a source of profound comfort in moments of temptation?

3. Explain the line 'One with himself I cannot die.' What does it mean to be 'one' with Jesus?

27 – *The Joy of Having a Perfect High Priest*

Reading: Romans 8:31-39

Arise, my soul, arise,	
Shake off thy guilty fears,	1 John 4:8
The bleeding sacrifice	
In my behalf appears;	Heb. 9:12
Before the throne my surety stands;	Heb. 7:22
My name is written on his hands.	
He ever lives above,	
For me to intercede;	Rom. 8:34
His all-redeeming love,	
His precious blood to plead:	1 John 1:7
His blood aton'd for all our race,	1 Tim. 2:6
And sprinkles now the throne of grace.	Heb. 10:22
Five bleeding wounds he bears,	
Receiv'd on Calvary;	
They pour effectual pray'rs,	
They strongly speak for me:	Heb. 12:24
Forgive him, O forgive they cry!	
Nor let that ransom'd sinner die.	
The Father hears him pray,	
His dear anointed one;	
He cannot turn away	
The presence of his Son:	
His spirit answers to the blood,	
And tells me I am born of God.	Rom. 8:16
My God is reconcil'd,	Rom 5:11
His pard'ning voice I hear;	
He owns me for his child,	
I can no longer fear;	Rom. 8:16
With confidence I now draw nigh,	Heb. 4;16
And Father, Abba Father, cry!	Gal. 4:6

CHARLES WESLEY

Reflection Questions:

1. When, during the act of repentance, is it appropriate to 'shake off' lingering feelings of guilt and fear?

2. The second-to-last stanza shows all three persons of the Trinity at work in forgiving a penitent sinner. What is the role of each person?

3. Why do you think that the hymn ends the way that it does? How is communion the final goal of repentance?

28 – *The Sympathy of Our High Priest*

Reading: Hebrews 4:14-16

With joy we meditate the grace
Of our High Priest above; Heb. 4:14
His heart is made of tenderness,
And ever yearns with love.

Touched with a sympathy within, Heb. 4:15
He knows our feeble frame;
He knows what sore temptations mean
For he has felt the same.

He in the days of feeble flesh
Poured out his cries and tears; Heb. 5:7
And, in his measure, feels afresh
What every member bears.

He'll never quench the smoking flax, Isa. 32:1-2
But raise it to a flame;
The bruisèd reed he never breaks,
Nor scorns the meanest name.

Then let our humble faith address
His mercy and his power: Heb. 4:16
We shall obtain delivering grace
In every needful hour.[1]

ISAAC WATTS

---

1 A wonderful hymn that treats a similar topic is 'There Is No Sorrow, Lord, Too Light' by Jane Crewdson.

Reflection Questions:

1. The book of Hebrews casts a spotlight on the sympathy of Jesus as our high priest (4:15; c.f. 2:17-18, 5:7-9). How should the sympathy of Christ affect our willingness to go to Him in prayer?

2. The hymn suggests that Christ 'feels afresh' the burden of a Christian. How does this thought comfort you?

3. Reread the final two lines of the hymn. What is 'delivering grace?' What is the difference between 'delivering grace' and 'pardoning grace?'

29 – *All Authority Has Been Given to Christ*

Reading: Psalm 72

Hail to the Lord's anointed,	
Great David's greater Son!	Ps. 110:1
Hail in the time appointed,	
His reign on earth begun!	1 Cor. 15:25
He comes to break oppression,	
To set the captive free;	Isa. 61:1
To take away transgression	
And rule in equity.	Ps. 72:1-4
He comes in succor speedy	
To those who suffer wrong;	
To help the poor and needy,	Ps. 72:12
And bid the weak be strong;	Joel 3:10
To give them songs for sighing,	Isa. 61:3
Their darkness turn to light,	Ps. 18:28, Isa. 60:1
Whose souls, condemned and dying,	
Were precious in His sight.	Ps. 72:14
By such shall He be fearèd	Ps. 72:5
While sun and moon endure;	
Beloved, obeyed, reverèd;	
For He shall judge the poor	
Through changing generations,	
With justice, mercy, truth,	
While stars maintain their stations,	
Or moons renew their youth.	
He shall come down like showers	Ps. 72:6
Upon the fruitful earth;	
Love, joy, and hope, like flowers,	
Spring in His path to birth.	
Before Him, on the mountains,	
Shall peace, the herald, go,	Isa. 52:7
And righteousness, in fountains,	
From hill to valley flow.	

Kings shall fall down before Him,
And gold and incense bring;   Isa. 61:4-7
All nations shall adore Him,
His praise all people sing;
For He shall have dominion   Ps. 72:8
O'er river, sea and shore,
Far as the eagle's pinion
Or dove's light wing can soar.

For Him shall prayer unceasing   Ps. 72:15
And daily vows ascend;
His kingdom still increasing,
A kingdom without end:
The mountain dews shall nourish
A seed in weakness sown,
Whose fruit shall spread and flourish
And shake like Lebanon.   Ps. 72:16

O'er every foe victorious,
He on His throne shall rest;
From age to age more glorious,
All blessing and all blest.   Ps. 72:18
The tide of time shall never
His covenant remove;   Isa. 55:3
His name shall stand forever,   Ps. 72:19
His name to us is Love.[1]

JAMES MONTGOMERY

---

1   Another exhilarating hymn on the ascension of Christ is Christopher Wordsworth's 'See, the Conqu'ror Mounts in Triumph.' The original gives a full typology of the ascension using numerous Old Testament figures.

Reflection Questions:

1. Like Isaac Watts's classic hymn 'Jesus Shall Reign,' this hymn is a long reflection on Psalm 72. How does the hymn demonstrate the fulfilment of the Psalm through the resurrection and ascension of Jesus?

2. Christians often forget that 'all authority' has been given to Christ (Matt. 28:18). How does the hymn remind us of the sovereign rule of Jesus *right now*?

3. How does this hymn affect your understanding of historical events and what is happening in the world right now?

30 – *The Authority of Christ in the Salvation of a Sinner*

Reading: Ephesians 2:1-10

And can it be that I should gain
An int'rest in the Savior's blood?
Died He for me, who caused His pain?
For me, who Him to death pursued?
Amazing love! how can it be
That Thou, my God, should die for me?

'Tis mystery all! Th'Immortal dies!
Who can explore His strange design?
In vain the firstborn seraph tries
To sound the depths of love divine!
'Tis mercy all! let earth adore,
Let angel minds inquire no more.   1 Pet. 1:12

He left His Father's throne above,
So free, so infinite His grace;
Emptied Himself of all but love,   Phil. 2:7
And bled for Adam's helpless race;   Rom. 5:12
'Tis mercy all, immense and free;
For, O my God, it found out me.

Long my imprisoned spirit lay   Isa. 61:1
Fast bound in sin and nature's night;
Thine eye diffused a quick'ning ray,   2 Cor. 4:6
I woke, the dungeon flamed with light;
My chains fell off, my heart was free;
I rose, went forth and followed Thee.

No condemnation now I dread;	Rom. 8:1
Jesus, and all in Him is mine!	Eph. 1:3, Col. 1:18
Alive in Him, my living Head,	Eph. 2:5
And clothed in righteousness divine,	Isa. 61:10
Bold I approach th'eternal throne,	Heb. 4:16
And claim the crown, through Christ	
my own.	2 Tim. 4:8

CHARLES WESLEY

Refection Questions:

1. Why does the hymn begin with a series of questions? What is the motive, or feeling, behind these questions?

2. What is the chain of events that leads to the prisoner in the hymn being set free (see the fourth stanza)?

3. How would you describe the attitude depicted in the final stanza? What is the difference between godly confidence and sinful presumption?

31 – The Authority of Christ in the Sanctification of a Christian

Reading: Ephesians 3:14-21

Love divine, all loves excelling,	
joy of heav'n, to earth come down,	
fix in us thy humble dwelling,	Eph. 3:17
all thy faithful mercies crown.	Ps. 103:4
Jesus, thou art all compassion,	
pure, unbounded love thou art.	Eph. 3:19
Visit us with thy salvation;	Ps. 85:7
enter ev'ry trembling heart.	Isa. 66:2

Breathe, O breathe thy loving Spirit	John 20:22
into ev'ry troubled breast.	
Let us all in thee inherit,	
let us find the promised rest.	Matt. 11:28
Take away the love of sinning;	
Alpha and Omega be.	Rev. 1:8
End of faith, as its beginning,	Rom. 1:17
set our hearts at liberty.	John 8:36

Come, Almighty, to deliver,
let us all thy life receive.
Suddenly return, and never,
nevermore they temples leave.
Thee we would be always blessing,
serve thee as thy hosts above,
pray, and praise thee without ceasing,
glory in thy perfect love.

Finish, then, thy new creation;　　　2 Cor. 5:17
true and spotless let us be.　　　　　Eph. 5:27
Let us see thy great salvation
perfectly restored in thee.
Changed from glory into glory,　　　2 Cor. 3:18
till in heav'n we take our place,
till we cast our crowns before thee,　Rev. 4:11
lost in wonder, love and praise.

CHARLES WESLEY

Reflection Questions:

1. How does this hymn reveal the work of Christ in sanctifying a believer?

2. What is the relationship between Jesus and the Holy Spirit in the hymn?

3. According to the final stanza, what is the ultimate goal of the work of sanctification?

32 – *The Authority of Christ in the Salvation of the Church*

Reading: Revelation 12:7-12

The church's one foundation	Eph. 2:20
Is Jesus Christ, her Lord;	1 Cor. 3:11
She is his new creation	Col. 1:18
By water and the Word:	Mark 16:16
From heav'n he came and sought her	
To be his holy bride;	John 3:29, Eph. 5:25
With his own blood he bought her,	
And for her life he died.	Rev. 5:9
Elect from ev'ry nation,	
Yet one o'er all the earth,	Rev. 5:9
Her charter of salvation	
One Lord, one faith, one birth;	Eph. 4:5
One holy name she blesses,	Acts 4:12, Phil. 2:8
Partakes one holy food,	John 6:27, 1 Cor. 11:24
And to one hope she presses,	
With ev'ry grace endued.	
Though with a scornful wonder	
Men see her sore oppressed,	
By schisms rent asunder,	
By heresies distressed,	
Yet saints their watch are keeping,	
Their cry goes up, "How long?"	Rev. 6:10
And soon the night of weeping	
Shall be the morn of song.	Ps. 30:5
The church shall never perish!	Matt. 16:18
Her dear Lord to defend,	
To guide, sustain, and cherish,	
Is with her to the end;	Matt. 28:20
Though there be those that hate her,	

And false sons in her pale,   Matt. 7:15
Against both foe and traitor
She ever shall prevail.

'Mid toil and tribulation,
And tumult of her war,   Gen. 3:15, Rev. 12:17
She waits the consummation
Of peace forevermore;   Isa. 2:4, Rev. 21:4
Till with the vision glorious
Her longing eyes are blest,   Rev. 22:4
And the great church victorious   Rev. 21:7
Shall be the church at rest.   Rev. 22:5

Yet she on earth hath union
With the God the Three in One,   2 Cor. 13:14
And mystic sweet communion
With those whose rest is won: Heb. 12:23
O happy ones and holy!
Lord, give us grace that we,
Like them, the meek and lowly,
On high may dwell with thee.

S. J. STONE

Reflection Questions:

1. Why is it important for us to not only think about the salvation of individual people, but also the salvation of the church as a whole?

2. This hymn is very honest about the warfare that the church endures in history. Still, the hymn is filled with hope. What is the source of the church's unwavering hope in the midst of suffering, false teaching, and moral failure?

3. How does the church fit into the ultimate purposes of God? Search the hymn and see what you find.

33 – Preparing for the Judgment of Christ

Reading: John 5:24-30

Thou judge of quick and dead, before whose bar severe,	Rom. 14:9, 2 Tim. 4:1
With holy joy, or guilty dread, we all shall soon appear;	1 Pet. 4:13, Isa. 2:10
Our cautioned souls prepare for that tremendous day,	1 Thess. 5:4, 1 Pet. 1:13
And fill us now with watchful care, and stir us up to pray.	Matt. 24:42-44, 25:13

To pray, and wait the hour, that wondrous hour unknown,	Matt. 24:36
When, robed in majesty and power, Thou shalt from Heaven come down	
The immortal Son of Man, to judge the human race,	Dan. 7:13-14
With all Thy Father's dazzling train, with all Thy glorious grace.	Matt. 24:30-31

To damp our earthly joys, to increase our gracious fears,	2 Cor. 5:11
For ever let the archangel's voice be sounding in our ears;	1 Thess. 4:16
The solemn midnight cry, Ye dead, the Judge is come,	1 Thess. 5:2
Arise, and meet Him in the sky, and meet your instant doom!	1 Thess. 4:17

O may we thus be found obedient
    to His Word,   Luke 12:43
Attentive to the trumpet's sound,
    and looking for our Lord!   Luke 12:36
O may we thus ensure a lot among
    the blest;
And watch a moment to secure an
    everlasting rest!   Heb. 4:9

CHARLES WESLEY

Reflection Questions:

1. Modern Christians do not spend much time meditating on the Day of Judgment. Why is this?

2. Look at the third line of the hymn. What does it mean to 'prepare for that tremendous day?' How do we prepare?[1]

3. Reread the third stanza. Why do we need our earthly joys to be dampened? Why do we need our gracious fears to be increased?

---

1   Two other hymns worth reading that reflect on the theme of judgment are 'Day of Judgment! Day of wonders!' and 'Oft as the Bell with Solemn Toll.' Both are by John Newton.

34 – The Dawning of the New Jerusalem

Reading: Revelation 21

Lo! what a glorious sight appears	
To our believing eyes!	Rom. 8:24
The earth and sea are passed away,	Rev. 21:1
And the old rolling skies.	Rev. 6:14
From the third heav'n, where God resides,	2 Cor. 12:2
That holy, happy place,	
The new Jerusalem comes down,	Rev. 21:2
Adorned with shining grace.	
Attending angels shout for joy,	
And the bright armies sing—	
"Mortals, behold the sacred seat	
Of your descending King.	
"The God of glory down to men	
Removes His blest abode;	Rev. 21:3
Men, the dear objects of His grace,	
And he the loving God.	
His own soft hand shall wipe the tears	
From every weeping eye,	Rev. 21:4
And pains, and groans, and griefs,	
* and fears,*	
And death itself, shall die.	1 Cor. 15:26, Isa. 25:8
How long, dear Savior! O how long	Rev. 6:10
Shall this bright hour delay?	
Fly swifter round, ye wheels of time,	
And bring the welcome day.	Rev. 22:20

Isaac Watts

Reflection Questions:

1. The tone of this hymn is very different than the previous one. Why is it important that Christians maintain both a joyful expectation and a fearful sober-mindedness as they anticipate the second coming of Jesus?

2. This hymn describes the joining of heaven and earth in the New Jerusalem (c.f. Revelation 21:10). What do you think life will be like in the New Jerusalem?

3. The final stanza says, 'How long, dear Savior!' Often, Christians are so content with this world that we never sigh and long for the coming of Christ. How do we break out of this premature contentment?

3

MEDITATING ON SPIRITUAL FELLOWSHIP

'That which we have seen and heard we proclaim also to you, so that you too may have fellowship with us; and indeed our fellowship is with the Father and with his Son Jesus Christ' (1 John 1:3).

It is one thing to know *about* God; it is something else to enjoy communion with God. Normal relationships illustrate this difference. I can read any number of biographies about a famous person such as the President of the United States. However, this information by itself will not result in a friendship. It would be absurd for me to say that I actually 'know' the President unless I've had the opportunity to meet him, spend time with him, and to share an exchange of feelings and ideas with him.

Christians must remember that Jesus did not come into the world to give us a scientific knowledge about God. He came so that we could be adopted as children into the divine family. Spiritual life is less about entering into erudite discussions about theology than it is about joining a dance of love and joy that has been going on since before the beginning.

Practically, this means that one of the great privileges of the Christian life is to grow in intimacy and communion with God. Such intimacy is defined not just by a knowledge of God in general, but a knowledge of Him according to each person of the Trinity. To know how to relate to the Father as Father, the Son as Son, and the Spirit as Spirit, is not just the benchmark of a high theological IQ. Such knowledge is a portal through which we can lovingly engage with the fullness of our Triune God.

Admittedly, the thought of learning how to fellowship with each member of the Trinity is intimidating. Most of us would not know where to begin in order to gain such knowledge. This is where hymns can be helpful. There are hymns that have been written with the goal in mind of teaching us about our relationships with different persons of the Trinity. These hymns are a gentle introduction to such knowledge. They enlighten the mind without overloading it with cumbersome debates and scholastic distinctions.

Now, the hymns in this section have been arranged into four groups. The first group focuses on fellowshipping with God the Father. Not enough Christians are aware of the degree to which Jesus' ministry is focused on giving us access to the Father Himself. The Scottish theologian Sinclair Ferguson writes, 'Jesus is the beam, but the Father himself is the sun of eternal love; Christ is the stream, but through him we are led to the Father who is the fountain of all grace and kindness.'[1] No Christian

---

1   See Sinclair Ferguson, *The Trinitarian Devotion of John Owen* (Sanford: Reformation Trust, 2014).

should be content unless he is drinking regularly from this fountain.

The second group is focused on fellowshipping with Jesus. These are some of the richest hymns in the entire collection. They focus broadly on two themes: the incomparable joy of knowing Christ and the spiritual benefits of communing with Jesus as our high priest.

The topic of the third group is fellowshipping with the Holy Spirit. This is an area of great confusion among contemporary Christians. These hymns are a broom for the mind. They will tidy up messy thinking regarding what the Spirit does and does not do. Of no small significance, they will remind us that the Spirit's primary job is not to lavish ecstatic gifts, but to unveil the glory of Christ (John 16:14).

Finally, loving God always results in loving one another. 1 John 3:14 says, 'We know that we have passed out of death into life, because we love the brothers.' With this in mind, a final set of hymns will describe the unique communion among believers, which is a byproduct of communion with God.

Fellowship with the Father

35 – The Glory of the Father

Reading: Isaiah 40:12-18

Immortal, invisible, God only wise,	1 Tim. 1:17
In light inaccessible hid from our eyes,	1 Tim. 6:15-16
Most blessed, most glorious, the Ancient of Days,	Dan. 7:9, 1 Tim. 1:11
Almighty, victorious, Thy great name we praise.	1 Chron. 29:11
Unresting, unhasting, and silent as light,	John 5:17, 1 John 1:5
Nor wanting, nor wasting, Thou rulest in might;	
Thy justice like mountains high soaring above	Ps. 36:6
Thy clouds which are fountains of goodness and love.	Isa. 45:8
To all life Thou givest, to both great and small;	Acts 17:25
In all life Thou livest, the true life of all;	Ps. 104:30
We blossom and flourish as leaves on the tree,	
And wither and perish, but nought changeth Thee.	Isa. 40:6-8

Great Father of Glory, pure Father of Light	James 1:17
Thine angels adore Thee, all veiling their sight;	Isa. 6:2
All laud we would render, O help us to see:	
'Tis only the splendor of light hideth Thee.	Ps. 104:2

WALTER CHALMERS SMITH

Reflection Questions:

1. How does this hymn invite us to have fellowship with our heavenly Father?

2. The second stanza mentions that God is 'unresting' and 'unhasting.' What does this mean?

3. How many attributes of God are mentioned in this hymn? Which one do you find particularly fascinating?

36 – The Mercy of the Father

Reading: 2 Corinthians 1:3-11

Thy mercy, my God, is the theme of my song,
The joy of my heart and the boast of my tongue;
Thy free grace alone, from the first to the last,
Hath won my affections and bound my soul fast.

Without thy free mercy I could not live here
Sin soon would reduce me to utter despair;
But, thro' thy free goodness, my spirits revive,   Isa. 57:15
And he that first made me, still keeps me alive.

Thy mercy surpasses the sin of my heart
Which wonders to feel its own hardness depart,
Dissolv'd by thy goodness, I fall to the ground
And weep to the praise of the mercy I found.

The door of thy mercy stands open all day   Matt. 7:7
To the needy and poor, who knock by the way;
No sinner shall ever be empty sent back,
Who comes seeking mercy for Jesus' dear sake.

Thy mercy in Jesus exempts me from hell;
Its glories I'll sing, and its wonders I'll tell:
'Twas Jesus my friend when he hung on the tree
That open'd the channel of mercy for me.

Great Father of mercies, thy goodness I own,   2 Cor. 1:3
And covenant love of thy crucify'd son:
All praise to the spirit, whose action divine
Seals mercy and pardon and righteousness
    mine.   Eph. 1:13

JOHN STOCKER

Reflection Questions:

1. We often think of God the Father as being harsh and overbearing. How does this hymn help us to overcome these assumptions?

2. How does the mercy of God affect the heart of the speaker in the hymn (see the third stanza)? When have you had a similar experience?

3. How can meditating on the mercy of God help us to have spiritual fellowship with God the Father?

37 – *The Kindness of the Father*

Reading: Psalm 23

The God of love my shepherd is,	1 John 4:16, Is. 40:11
And he that doth me feed;	
While he is mine and I am his,	Song 6:3
What can I want or need?	Ps. 23:1, Ps. 34:10
He leads me to the tender grass,	
Where I both feed and rest;	
Then to the streams that gently pass:	
In both I have the best.	Ps. 23:2
Or if I stray, he doth convert,	
And bring my mind in frame,	
And all this not for my desert,	
But for his holy name.	Ps. 23:3
Yea, in death's shady black abode	
Well may I walk, not fear;	
For thou art with me, and thy rod	
To guide, thy staff to bear.	Ps. 23:4
Surely thy sweet and wondrous love	
Shall measure all my days;	
And, as it never shall remove,	Isa. 54:10
So neither shall my praise.	Ps. 34:1

GEORGE HERBERT

Reflection Questions:

1. How does a picture of a gentle and kind shepherd help us to reimagine the fatherhood of God?

2. What difference does it make that God's love is motivated by 'his holy name' rather than by 'my desert?'

3. This hymn speaks of God providing us with the 'the best.' What does this mean? How can having what is 'best' be different from getting what we want?

38 – The Sheer Delight of Knowing the Father

Reading: Psalm 16:5-11

My God, my life, my love,
To thee, to thee I call;
I cannot live if thou remove,
For thou art all in all.   Eph. 1:23, 1 Cor. 15:28

Thy shining grace can cheer
This dungeon where I dwell;
'Tis paradise when thou art here;
If thou depart, 'tis hell.

The smilings of thy face,
How amiable they are!
'Tis heaven to rest in thine embrace;   Song 2:6
And nowhere else but there.

To thee, and thee alone,
The angels owe their bliss;   Ps. 148:2
They sit around thy gracious throne,
And dwell where Jesus is.   Rev. 5:11

Not all the harps above
Can make a heavenly place,
If God his residence remove,
Or but conceal his face.   Ps. 143:7

Nor earth, nor all the sky,
Can one delight afford,
Nor yield one drop of real joy,
Without thy presence, Lord.   Ps. 73:25

Thou art the sea of love,
Where all my pleasures roll;   Ps. 16:11
The circle where my passions move,
And center of my soul.

ISAAC WATTS

Reflection Questions:

1. Why do we struggle to believe that God the Father is the source of pleasure? What spiritual biases do we have that influence our attitudes toward the Father?

2. Read the second to last stanza. Do you believe, *really believe*, that all real joy depends on the presence of God? Why or why not?

3. Reread the final stanza, line by line. What is the hymn writer saying? Put this stanza in your own words.[1]

---

1 Two other hymns to use to deepen fellowship with the Father, both found in this book, are 'My God, How Wonderful Thou Art' and 'Twas Not to Make Jehovah's Love.'

Fellowship with Jesus

39 – Thou We Have Not Seen Jesus, We Love Him

Reading: 1 Peter 1:3-8

Jesus, these eyes have never seen	
That radiant form of thine;	Matt. 17:2
The veil of sense hangs dark between	
Thy blessed face and mine.	2 Cor. 5:6-7

I see thee not, I hear thee not,	
Yet art thou oft with me;	Matt. 28:20
And earth hath ne'er so dear a spot	
As where I meet with thee.	Ps. 63:1

Like some bright dream that comes unsought
When slumbers o'er me roll,
Thine image ever fills my thought
And charms my ravished soul.

Yet, though I have not seen, and still	
Must rest in faith alone,	Rom. 8:24-25
I love thee, dearest Lord, and will,	
Unseen, but not unknown.	1 Pet. 1:8

When death these mortal eyes shall seal,	
And still this throbbing heart,	
The rending veil shall thee reveal,	Heb. 10:20
All glorious as thou art.	1 John 3:20

Ray Palmer

Reflection Questions:

1. What does it mean that Jesus is 'Unseen, but not unknown?'

2. What do you think it will be like to see Jesus one day 'All glorious as thou art?'

3. How does this hymn help us to think about what it means to have fellowship with Jesus?

40 – The Sweetness of Christ's Presence

Reading: Psalm 45:2-11

Jesus, the very thought of Thee
With sweetness fills the breast;
But sweeter far Thy face to see,
And in Thy presence rest.

Nor voice can sing, nor heart can frame,
Nor can the memory find
A sweeter sound than Thy blest name,
O Savior of mankind!

O hope of every contrite heart,	Isa. 66:2
O joy of all the meek,	Matt. 5:5
To those who fall, how kind Thou art!	Ps. 37:24
How good to those who seek!	Jer. 29:13

But what to those who find? Ah, this	
Nor tongue nor pen can show;	Ps. 45:1
The love of Jesus, what it is,	
None but His loved ones know.	Rev. 2:17

Jesus, our only joy be Thou,	
As Thou our prize will be;	
Jesus be Thou our glory now,	Gal. 6:14
And through eternity.	

O Jesus, King most wonderful	
Thou Conqueror renowned,	Rev. 19:11
Thou sweetness most ineffable	
In whom all joys are found!	

When once Thou visitest the heart,   Rev. 3:20
Then truth begins to shine,
Then earthly vanities depart,
Then kindles love divine.[1]

BERNARD OF CLAIRVAUX, *Trans.* EDWARD CASWALL

Reflection Questions:

1. Read the first stanza. What does it mean to rest in the presence of Jesus?

2. The hymn describes a secret pleasure that 'None but his loved ones know.' Think back to a moment when you had a special taste of the love of Jesus. How would you describe your experience?

3. Reread the final stanza. What does it mean for truth 'to shine?' Why does this experience cause 'earthly vanities' to depart?

---

1 There are further verses to this hymn which are equally beautiful and ravishing.

41 – Your Presence Makes My Paradise

Reading: Song of Solomon 1:1-4

Jesus hath died that I might live,	Rom. 14:9
Might live to God alone;	
In Him eternal life receive,	John 3:16
And be in spirit one.	John 17:22

Savior, I thank thee for the grace,
The gift unspeakable:
And wait with arms of faith t'embrace,
And all Thy love to feel.

My soul breaks out in strong desire	Ps. 63:1
The perfect bliss to prove;	
My longing heart is all on fire	
To be dissolved in love.	Song 1:1

Give me thyself; from every boast,	
From every wish set free;	
Let all I am in thee be lost,	Phil. 3:8
But give Thyself to me.	Song 8:6

Thy gifts, alas! cannot suffice	
Unless Thyself be given;	
Thy presence makes my paradise,	
And where Thou art is heaven.[1]	Ps. 84:1-2

CHARLES WESLEY

---

1 Another wonderful hymn, similar to this one, is 'Compared with Christ, in All Beside' by Augustus Toplady.

Reflection Questions:

1. How would you describe the emotion of the third stanza? Does this stanza resonate with your own desires?

2. The fourth stanza says, 'Give me thyself.' What does this mean? What does it mean for Jesus to give Himself to us?

3. Look at the final stanza. Why can't the gifts of Christ replace Christ Himself? What is supremely good about Christ Himself?

42 – Jesus, Thou Art All

Readings: Galatians 2:20, Romans 6:4-10

O Jesus Christ, grow Thou in me,	Gal. 4:19
And all things else recede!	
My heart be daily nearer Thee,	
From sin be daily freed.	Rom. 6:14

Each day let Thy supporting might	
My weakness still embrace;	2 Cor. 12:10
My darkness vanish in Thy light,	
Thy life my death efface.	

In Thy bright beams which on me fall,	
Fade every evil thought:	2 Cor. 4:6
That I am nothing, Thou art all,	Col. 1:18
I would be daily taught.	

More of Thy glory let me see,	Exod. 33:18
Thou holy, wise and true!	
I would Thy living image be,	2 Cor. 3:18
In joy and sorrow, too.	

Fill me with gladness from above,
Hold me by strength divine;
Lord, make the glow of Thy great love
Through my whole being shine.

Make this poor self grow less and less,	
Be Thou my life and aim;	Phil. 3:14
O make me daily through Thy grace,	
More meet to bear Thy name!	

Johann Kaspar Lavater

Reflection Questions:

1. If you had to summarize the message of this hymn in one sentence, what would it be?

2. Galatians 2:20 is one of the great verses in the Bible. How is this hymn a commentary on that verse?

3. The hymn says, 'Be Thou my life and aim.' What does it mean for Jesus to be both our life and our aim?

43 – To See Thee Is to Praise Thee

Reading: John 10:11-18

How sweet the Name of Jesus sounds
In a believer's ear!
It soothes his sorrow, heals his wounds,
And drives away his fear.

It makes the wounded spirit whole,
And calms the troubled breast;
'Tis manna to the hungry soul,   John 6:32-33
And to the weary, rest.   Matt. 11:28-30

Dear Name, the rock on which I build,   Ps. 61:2
My shield and hiding place,   Ps. 28:7, 32:7
My never failing treasury, filled
With boundless stores of grace!   Eph. 3:8

By Thee, my prayers acceptance gain,
Although with sin defiled;
Satan accuses me in vain,   Rom. 8:31
And I am owned a child.

Jesus, my Shepherd, Brother, Friend,   John 10:14, 15:15
My Prophet, Priest, and King,   Heb. 1:1-3
My Lord, my life, my way, my end,   1 Cor. 1:30
Accept the praise I bring.

Weak is the effort of my heart,
And cold my warmest thought;
But when I see Thee as Thou art,   1 John 3:2
I'll praise Thee as I ought.

'Til then I would Thy love proclaim
With every fleeting breath,
And may the music of Thy name
Refresh my soul in death.

JOHN NEWTON

Reflection Questions:

1. Reread the first two stanzas. What is the effect of the name of Jesus on the heart of a believer?

2. Look at the fifth stanza. Take note of all the roles that Jesus fulfills for us. Which roles do you need to be reminded of right now?

3. Consider the following line: 'When I see Thee as Thou art,/I'll praise Thee as I ought.' What is the connection between sight and praise?

44 – Communing with Jesus as High Priest

Reading: Hebrews 4:14-16

Approach, my soul, the mercy-seat,	Heb. 10:22
Where Jesus answers pray'r;	
There humbly fall before his feet,	Rev. 1:17
For none can perish there.	John 3:16

Thy promise is my only plea,
With this I venture nigh;
Thou callest burden'd souls to thee,   1 Pet. 5:7
And such, O Lord, am I.

Bow'd down beneath a load of sin,
By Satan sorely prest,   2 Cor. 4:8
By wars without, and fears within,   2 Cor. 7:5
I come to thee for rest.   Matt. 11:28

Be thou my shield and hiding place!   Ps. 119:114
That, shelter'd near thy side,
I may my fierce accuser face,
And tell him, thou hast dy'd.   Rom. 8:34

O wond'rous love! to bleed and die,
To bear the cross and shame;   Heb. 12:2
That guilty sinners such as I,
Might plead thy gracious name.

"Poor tempest-tossed soul be still,
My promis'd grace receive;"
'Tis Jesus speaks, I must, I will,
I can, I do believe.[1]

JOHN NEWTON

---

1   A similar hymn that is useful to read beside this one is 'Heal Us, Emmanuel, Hear Our Prayer' by William Cowper.

Reflection Questions:

1. What is the condition of the speaker as he draws near to Jesus in the hymn?

2. What defense does the speaker use against the accusations of Satan? What can we learn from this?

3. Reflect on the final stanza. Who speaks at the start of this stanza? What is the result of these words?

45 – *Fleeing to Jesus in Moments of Need*

Reading: Mark 4:35-41

Jesu, lover of my soul,
Let me to thy bosom fly,
While the nearer waters roll,　　　Ps. 69:2
While the tempest still is high;
Hide me, O my Saviour, hide,　　　Ps. 27:5
Till the storm of life is past;
Safe into the haven guide,　　　Ps. 107:30
O receive my soul at last!

Other refuge have I none,　　　Ps. 142:4
Hangs my helpless soul on thee;
Leave, ah! leave me not alone,
Still support and comfort me:
All my trust on thee is stay'd,　　　Ps. 31:14
All mine help from thee I bring,
Cover my defenseless head
With the shadow of thy wing.　　　Ps. 91:4

Thou, O Christ, art all I want,　　　Phil. 1:21
More than all in thee I find;
Raise the fallen, cheer the faint,　　　Isa. 40:29
Heal the sick, and lead the blind:
Just and holy is thy name;
I am all unrighteousness;　　　Isa. 1:6
False, and full of sin I am,
Thou art full of truth and grace.　　　John 1:17

Plenteous grace with thee is found,
Grace to cover all my sin:
Let the healing streams abound;   Ezek. 47
Make and keep me pure within.   Ezek. 47:8
Thou of life the fountain art,   Ps. 36:9
Freely let me take of thee;   Isa. 55:1
Spring thou up within mine heart,   John 7:37-39
Rise to all eternity.

Reflection Questions:

1. Reread the first stanza. What does it mean to fly to the bosom of Jesus? When should we fly to the bosom of Jesus?

2. How does the hymn depict the relationship between Jesus and the believer? What does Jesus bring to this relationship? What do we bring to this relationship?

3. The hymn begins by calling Jesus the 'lover of my soul.' What tricks does Satan use to make us doubt the love that Jesus has for us?

Fellowship with the Holy Spirit

46 – *The Majesty of the Spirit*

Readings: Exodus 40:34-38; 1 Corinthians 3:16-17

The Holy Ghost is here,	
Where saints in prayer agree,	Matt. 18:20
As Jesus' parting gift is near	John 14:18
Each pleading company.	

Not far away is He,
To be by prayer brought nigh,
But here in present majesty,
As in His courts on high.   Eph. 3:16-17

He dwells within our soul,   1 Cor. 3:16
An ever welcome guest;
He reigns with absolute control,
As monarch in the breast.

Our bodies are His shrine,   1 Cor. 6:19
And He th'indwelling Lord;   2 Cor. 3:17
All hail, Thou Comforter divine,   John 14:16
Be evermore adored.

Obedient to Thy will,
We wait to feel Thy power;   Acts 1:8
O Lord of life, our hopes fulfill,
And bless this hallowed hour.

Charles Spurgeon

Reflection Questions:

1. A lot of Christians think of the Spirit as shy and timid. How does this hymn correct this misconception?

2. What comfort should it bring us that '[The Spirit] reigns with absolute control,/As monarch in the breast?'

3. The Bible is clear that our bodies are the 'shrine', or temple, of the Holy Spirit. How should knowledge of this truth affect us?

47 – The Unique Gifts of the Spirit

Readings: John 14:15-18, 16:5-15

Come, holy celestial Dove,	Matt. 3:16
To visit a sorrowful breast,	2 Cor. 7:10
My burden of guilt to remove,	Rom. 8:1-2
And bring me assurance and rest:	Rom. 8:15

Thou only hast pow'r to relieve
A sinner o'erwhelmed with his load;
The sense of acceptance to give, — Rom. 8:16
And sprinkle his heart with thy blood. — Ezek. 36:25-26

With me if of old thou hast strove, — James 4:5
And strangely with-held from my sin,
And try'd, by the lure of thy love,
My worthless affections to win: — 2 Cor. 3:18

The work of thy mercy revive;
Thy uttermost mercy exert;
And kindly continue to strive, — Gal. 5:17
And hold till I yield thee my heart. — Luke 1:38

Thy call if I ever have known, — John 3:8
And sigh'd from myself to get free; — Rom. 7:24
And groan'd the unspeakable groan, — Rom. 8:26
And long'd to be happy in thee:

Fulfil the imperfect desire,
Thy peace to my conscience reveal,
The sense of thy favour inspire,
And give me my pardon to feel! — John 16:13-15

If, when I have put thee to grief, — Eph. 4:30
And madly to folly return'd, — Prov. 26:11
Thy pity has been my relief,
And lifted me up as I mourn'd:

Most pitiful Spirit of Grace,
Relieve me again, and restore;
My spirit in holiness raise,   Rom. 1:4
To fall and to suffer no more.

If now I lament after God,   Ps. 42:1
And gasp for a drop of thy love,
If Jesus hath bought thee with blood,
For me to receive from above: Gal. 3:14

Come, heav'nly Comforter, come,
True witness of mercy divine,   John 14:17, 16:13
And make me thy permanent home, John 14:16
And seal me eternally thine!   Eph. 1:13

CHARLES WESLEY

Reflection Questions:

1. A lot of Christians are uncertain about the role of the Spirit in the salvation of believers. What roles are highlighted in this hymn?

2. This hymn is written as a prayer to the Holy Spirit. When should we pray directly to the Holy Spirit?

3. Read John 16:14. What do you think this verse means? What does it reveal about the work of the Spirit?

48 – The Spirit's Gift of Assurance

Reading: Romans 8:9-17

I WANT the Spirit of power within,	2 Tim. 1:7
Of love, and of a healthful mind;	
Of power, to conquer inbred sin,	Rom. 8:13
Of love, to thee and all mankind,	Rom. 5:5, 1 Cor. 12:13
Of health, that pain and death defies,	
Most vigorous when the body dies.	1 Cor. 15:44
When shall I hear the inward voice	Rom. 8:27
Which only faithful souls can hear?	1 Cor. 2:12-14
Pardon, and peace, and heavenly joys	
Attend the promised Comforter;	John 14:16
O come, and righteousness divine,	Rom. 8:10
And Christ, and all with Christ,	John 16:14-16
are mine!	Rom. 8:16-17
O that the Comforter would come!	
Nor visit as a transient guest,	Ps. 51:11
But fix in me his constant home,	John 14:16
And take possession of my breast,	
And fix in me his loved abode,	
The temple of indwelling God!	1 Cor. 6:19
Come, Holy Ghost, my heart inspire!	
Attest that I am born again;	Rom. 8:16, Titus 3:5
Come, and baptize me now with fire,	Matt. 3:11, Acts 2:3
Nor let thy former gifts be vain;	
I cannot rest in sins forgiven,	
Where is the earnest of my heaven?	2 Cor. 1:23

Where the indubitable seal
That ascertains the kingdom mine?
The powerful stamp I long to feel,
The signature of love divine;   2 Cor. 3:3
O shed it in my heart abroad,   Rom. 5:5
Fullness of love, of heaven, of God!   Eph. 3:19

CHARLES WESLEY

Reflection Questions:

1. Read 2 Timothy 1:7. How is the first stanza a commentary on this verse?

2. What is the role of the Spirit in enabling Christians to have assurance of salvation?

3. The last stanza speaks of 'the signature of love divine.' What is the significance of a signature? What is the relationship between the work of the Holy Spirit and 'the signature of love divine?'

49 – *The Intimacy of Communion with the Holy Spirit*

Reading: 1 Corinthians 2:6-16

O breath of God, breathe on us now	Gen. 1:2
And move within us while we pray;	Acts 2:2
You are the spring of our new life,	John 3:5, Titus 3:5
The very light of our new day.	1 Pet. 2:9
How strangely you are with us, Lord,	John 3:8
Neither in height nor depth to seek:	Rom. 10:6-7
In nearness shall your voice be heard;	Rom. 10:8
Spirit to spirit you will speak.	Rom. 8:16
Christ is our advocate on high;	Rom. 8:34
You are our advocate within:	John 14:16
O plead the truth, and make reply	Rom. 8:15
To every argument of sin.	
But what a faithless heart of mine:	
The way I know, I know my guide:	
Forgive me, O my friend divine,	
That I so often turn aside.	
Be with me when no other friend	
The mystery of my heart can share;	Rom. 8:26-27
Be always known, when fears descend,	
By your best name of Comforter.	John 14:16

ALFRED VINE

Reflection Questions:

1. What does it mean that the Spirit speaks to us 'Spirit to spirit' (see the second stanza)?

2. Why do we need an 'advocate on high' and an 'advocate within?'

3. Read the final line of the stanza. Why is 'Comforter' the 'best name' of the Spirit?

50 – The Holy Spirit Inspires Worship

Reading: Leviticus 9:22-29

Come, Holy Spirit, heavenly Dove,	Gen. 8:11, Luke 3:22
With all thy quickening powers;	Isa. 32:15
Kindle a flame of sacred love	
In these cold hearts of ours.	Lev. 9:24

Behold us groveling here below,
Engag'd in trifling toys!
Our souls can neither fly, nor go
To reach eternal joys.

In vain we tune our formal songs,	Isa. 29:13
In vain we strive to rise;	
Hosannah's languish on our tongues,	Matt. 21:10
And our devotion dies.	

Dear Lord! and shall we still remain	
In this declining state?	
Our love so faint, so cold to thee,	Rev. 2:4
And thine to us so great?	

Come, Holy Spirit, heavenly Dove,	
With all thy quickening powers;	
Come, shed abroad a Saviour's love	Rom. 5:5
And that shall kindle ours.	

Isaac Watts

Reflection Questions:

1. Describe the condition of the heart of the speaker of this hymn. Can you identify with this condition?

2. Look at the last stanza. What is required to kindle a heart of worship?

3. If we keep the message of this hymn in mind, what should we do when our devotion feels formal, cold, and lifeless?

Fellowship with One Another

51 – The Communion of Saints

Reading: John 15:12-17

He wants not friends that hath Thy love,	John 15:15
And may converse and walk with Thee;	2 Cor. 6:16-18
And with Thy saints here and above,	
With whom forever I must be.	
In the communion of the saints	Heb. 12:1
Is wisdom, safety and delight;	
And, when my heart declines and faints,	Heb. 10:24-25
It's raised by their heat and light.	Eccles. 4:9-12
As for my friends, they are not lost;	1 Thess. 4:13
The several vessels of Thy fleet,	
Though parted now, by tempests tossed,	
Shall safely in the haven meet.	1 Thess. 4:17
Still we are centered all in Thee,	1 John 1:3
Members, though distant, of one head;	1 Cor. 12:12, Col. 1:18
In the same family we be,	Eph. 2:19, Gal. 3:28
By the same faith and Spirit led.	Eph. 4:4-5
Before Thy throne we daily meet	
As joint petitioners to Thee;	Heb. 4:16
In spirit we each other greet,	Col. 2:5
And shall again each other see.	1 Thess. 4:16-18
The heav'nly hosts, world without end,	
Shall be my company above;	Heb. 12:22-23
And Thou, my best and surest Friend,	
Who shall divide me from Thy love?[1]	Rom. 8:35

Richard Baxter

---

1   For a powerful hymn on how the church militant can learn the song of the church triumphant, see James Montgomery's 'Sing We the Song of Those Who Stand.'

Reflection Questions:

1. How is there 'wisdom, safety, and delight' in the fellowship of believers? Consider each word in particular.

2. C. S. Lewis once said that there are no goodbyes among Christians. How does the third stanza depict this cheerful truth?

3. How does our fellowship as Christians extend beyond the limits of space and time?

52 – Joint Pilgrims on the Road to Glory

Reading: Philippians 1:27-30

Thou God of truth and love,	
We seek thy perfect way,	
Ready thy choice t' approve,	Luke 1:38
Thy providence t' obey,	
Enter into thy wise design,	
And sweetly lose our will in thine.	John 4:34

Why hast thou cast our lot
In the same age and place?
And why together brought
To see each other's face;
To join with softest sympathy,
And mix our friendly souls in thee?

Didst thou not make us one,	John 17:21-23
That we might one remain,	
Together travel on,	
And bear each other's pain,	Gal. 6:2
Till all thy utmost goodness prove,	
And rise renew'd in perfect love?	

Surely thou didst unite	
Our kindred spirits here,	
That all hereafter might	
Before thy throne appear;	
Meet at the marriage of the Lamb,	Rev. 19:7-9
And all thy glorious love proclaim.	Ps. 118:17

Then let us ever bear	
The blessed end in view,	Ps. 84:2, 137:6
And join with mutual care,	
To fight our passage through;	2 Cor. 10:3, Eph. 6:11
And kindly help each other on,	
Till all receive thy starry crown.	James 1:12

O may thy Spirit seal	
Our souls unto that day!	Eph. 4:30
With all thy fulness fill,	Eph. 3:19
And then transport away!	
Away to our eternal rest,	Heb. 4:10
Away to our Redeemer's breast!	John 21:20

CHARLES WESLEY

Reflection Questions:

1. We often take for granted the Christians around us. How does the second stanza remind us that our Christian communities are a product of divine sovereignty?

2. The hymn is built on the image of a band of pilgrims traveling together. Look at the fourth stanza. What is our final destination? Why is it important to keep this destination in view?

3. The hymn talks about the need to help each other 'fight our passage through.' What do we need to fight against as we journey together toward the marriage supper of the Lamb?

53 – *Bond of Perfection*

Reading: 1 Corinthians 12:12-22

Jesus, united by Thy grace,	Rom. 15:5-6
And each to each endeared,	Phil. 1:7-8
With confidence we seek Thy face	1 Chron. 28:9
And know our prayer is heard.	John 14:13, Ps. 34:15

Still let us own our common Lord,	Eph. 4:5
And bear Thine easy yoke,	Matt. 11:29
A band of love, a threefold cord,	Eccles. 4:12
Which never can be broke.	

Make us into one spirit drink;	1 Cor. 12:13
Baptize into Thy name;	
And let us always kindly think,	Phil. 2:2-3
And sweetly speak, the same.	

Help us to help each other, Lord,	
Each other's cross to bear;	Gal. 6:2
Let all their friendly aid afford,	
And feel each other's care.	1 Cor. 12:25-27

Up onto Thee, our living Head,	
Let us in all things grow;	Eph. 4:15
Till Thou hast made us free indeed	
And spotless here below.	Jude 1:24

Touched by the lodestone[1] of Thy love,	
Let all our hearts agree,	John 17:21
And ever toward each other move,	
And ever move toward Thee.	

---

1   A loadstone is a naturally occurring magnet that can attract other minerals to itself.

To Thee, inseparably joined,   Eph. 4:16
Let all our spirits cleave;
O may we all the loving mind,
That was in Thee receive.   Phil. 2:2

This is the bond of perfectness,   Col. 3:14
Thy spotless charity;
O let us, still we pray, possess
The mind that was in Thee.   Phil. 2:5

CHARLES WESLEY

Reflection Questions:

1. According to the hymn, how should our relationship with Christ affect our relationships with one another?

2. What does it mean to be 'Touched by the lodestone of Thy love?' How does the touch of God's love cause our hearts to be attracted to one another?

3. Read Philippians 2:5. How does this hymn help us to understand the meaning of this verse?

4

Meditating on Spiritual Transformation

Spiritual transformation requires two things. The first is a change of deep and often hidden motives of the heart. If we love wrongly, we live wrongly. This is one of the most basic and unchangeable rules of human behavior. The second requirement is a slow growth in virtue. There are no shortcuts to mature character. Old habits must tirelessly be put to death, and new habits – those reflecting the nature of Jesus – must, with equal resolve, be put on. The end goal of this process is nothing less than a radical reshaping of the self. Increasingly, we hope to bear an unmistakable family resemblance to God Himself. Our longing is that, when people see us, they in fact see *through us*. The height of sanctity is being a clear and spotless window that puts the beauty of divine holiness on display to the world.

The hymns in this section focus on these two areas of change. The first set describes the kind of affections that underlie a life devoted to godliness. They speak of love and gratitude, in particular, in a way that will both challenge and inspire the reader. Such hymns should not primarily be used as a diagnostic test for the spiritual health of our hearts. To hold ourselves to such ideal standards will result in frustration and despair, not encouragement and hope. We ought to read these hymns, not so much as descriptions of 'where I *ought* to be,' as statements of 'where I *can* begin to go.' Put differently, these hymns identify some of the grand peaks of godliness, which, over time – and by the grace of God – normal people like us can begin to climb.

The second set focuses on some of the most important virtues of godly character. The portrait sketched by these hymns will not be comprehensive. Many other hymns could be added to fill in gaps in the picture. However, our goal here is not to be exhaustive, but to be selective. These hymns have been chosen, in particular, because they challenge some of the moral weaknesses that are endemic among modern Christians.

Finally, something should be said about the placement of this section of hymns. This group purposely comes after the first two sets of spiritual exercises, which are on the topics of understanding the gospel and communion with God. There is a reason for this. The gospel is not just the unique means of salvation; it is also the unique means of sanctification. There would be a grave danger of self-reliance or self-righteousness if our exercises on holy character came before a clear statement of the person and work of Jesus. We need to be absolutely clear about the following point: The only way to grow in godliness is by setting the eyes of faith on the person of Jesus Christ.

Likewise, communion with God is not just a spiritual perk of being saved. Knowing God and being transformed into His image are inextricably linked. Perhaps the clearest statement of this connection is found in 2 Corinthians 3:18. Paul writes, 'And we all, with unveiled face, beholding the glory of the Lord, are being transformed into the same image from one degree of glory to another' (ESV). In Paul's thinking, seeing and changing are two stages of a single experience. What we worship is what we become.

Thus, we see that the combination of trusting in the gospel and walking in communion with God is the surest road to holiness. It is only by following this path that the commandment will progressively be fulfilled, 'You shall be holy, for I am holy' (1 Pet. 1:16; c.f. Lev. 11:44).

54 – *The Spiritual Power of Beauty*

Reading: 2 Corinthians 3:15-18

Now let us see Thy beauty, Lord,   2 Cor. 3:18
As we have seen before;
And by Thy beauty quicken us
To love Thee and adore.

'Tis easy when with simple mind
Thy loveliness we see,
To consecrate ourselves afresh
To duty and to Thee.   Ps. 27:4

Our every feverish mood is cooled,
And gone is every load,
When we can lose the love of self,
And find the love of God.   John 3:30

'Tis by Thy loveliness we're won
To home and Thee again,
And as we are Thy children true
We are more truly men.   Eph. 4:24

Lord, it is coming to ourselves   Luke 15:17
When thus we come to Thee;
The bondage of Thy loveliness
Is perfect liberty.   2 Cor. 3:17

So now we come to ask again,
What Thou hast often giv'n,
The vision of that loveliness
Which is the life of Heav'n.   Rev. 22:3-5

BENJAMIN WAUGH

Reflection Questions:

1. Reread the first line. What does it mean to see the beauty of God?

2. Look at each stanza: What are the spiritual effects of encountering the beauty of God?

3. Reread the final two lines. Try to put these lines in your own words. In what sense is a vision of beauty 'the life of Heav'n?'

55 – Love: Our Highest Motive

Reading: 1 Corinthians 13:1-3

Happy the Heart where Graces reign,	Rom. 5:21
Where Love inspires the Breast,	
Love is the brightest of the Train,[1]	
And strengthens all the rest.	

Knowledge, alas! 'tis all in vain,	1 Cor. 8:1
And all in vain our Fear,	Rom. 8:15
Our stubborn Sins will fight and reign,	
If Love be absent there.	

'Tis Love that makes our cheerful Feet	
In swift Obedience move,	
The Devils know and tremble too,	James 2:19
But Satan cannot love.	

This is the Grace that lives and sings,	
When Faith and Hope shall cease;	1 Cor. 13:13
'Tis this shall strike our joyful Strings	
In the Sweet Realms of bliss.	

Before we quite forsake our Clay,
Or leave this dark Abode,
The Wings of Love bear us away
To see our smiling God.
Isaac Watts

---

1   'Train' is meant here in the sense of an ordered series of things.

Reflection Questions:

1. The first stanza says that love strengthens all of the other graces. What does this mean?

2. What does it mean that love 'makes our cheerful feet/ In swift obedience move?'

3. Look at the final line of the hymn. In what sense does God smile? How does love enable us to see 'our smiling God?'

56 – *Teach Me to Love You More*

Reading: John 21:15-19

Do not I love Thee, O my Lord?   James 21:15
Behold my heart and see;
And turn each cursèd idol out,
That dares to rival Thee.

Do not I love Thee, O my Lord?
Then let me nothing love;
Dead be my heart to every joy,
When Jesus cannot move.

Is not Thy name melodious still
To mine attentive ear?
Doth not each pulse with pleasure bound
My Savior's voice to hear?

Hast Thou a lamb in all Thy flock
I would disdain to feed?   John 21:15
Hast Thou a foe, before whose face
I fear Thy cause to plead?

Would not mine ardent spirit vie
With angels round the throne,
To execute Thy sacred will,   Heb. 1:7, Ps. 104:4
And make Thy glory known?

Would not my heart pour forth its blood
In honor of Thy name?
And challenge the cold hand of death
To damp th'immortal flame?

Thou know'st I love Thee, dearest Lord,
But O, I long to soar
Far from the sphere of mortal joys,
And learn to love Thee more!

PHILLIP DODDERIDGE

Reflection Questions:

1. How many rhetorical questions are included in this hymn? Why does the hymn make so much use of this form of speech?

2. How does your heart compare to the heart of the speaker in the hymn? Do you feel the same spiritual ardor and thirst, which is communicated through the hymn?

3. What should we do when our love begins to feel cold? How can we 'learn to love Thee more?'

57 – The Giver Is Greater than the Gifts

Reading: 1 John 4:7-11

My God, I love Thee; not because	
I hope for heav'n thereby,	
Nor yet for fear that loving not	
I might forever die;	
But for that Thou didst all mankind	
Upon the cross embrace;	1 Tim. 2:6
For us didst bear the nails and spear,	
And manifold disgrace;	Heb. 12:2
And griefs and torments numberless,	
And sweat of agony;	Luke 22:44
Even death itself, and all for man,	
Who was Thine enemy.	Rom. 5:8
Then why, most loving Jesus Christ,	
Should I not love Thee well?	1 John 3:16
Not for the sake of winning heav'n,	
Nor any fear of hell;	

Not with the hope of gaining aught,[1]
Nor seeking a reward,
But as Thyself hast loved me,
O ever loving Lord!
E'en so I love Thee, and will love,
And in Thy praise will sing,
Solely because Thou art my God
And my eternal King!

FRANCIS XAVIER

---

1   Anything

Reflection Questions:

1. The Bible talks a lot about the fear of the Lord. How should love and fear go together in the heart of faith?

2. The Bible also talks a lot about rewards. How should love and the incentive of rewards go together in the heart of faith?

3. According to the hymn, what is the ultimate reason that we should love God?[2]

---

2   Anyone interested in thinking deeply about this topic should read Bernard of Clairvaux's classic work, *On Loving God.*

58 – Love Orders the Heart

Reading: Psalm 84:10-12

Let worldly minds the world pursue,	1 John 2:15-17
It has no charms for me;	
Once I admired its trifles too,	
But grace has set me free.	Gal. 4:9, 5:1

Its pleasures now no longer please,
No more content afford;
Far from my heart be joys like these;
Now I have seen the Lord.   John 20:18

As by the light of opening day
The stars are all concealed;
So earthly pleasures fade away,
When Jesus is revealed.

Creatures no more divide my choice,   Ps. 86:11
I bid them all depart;
His name, and love, and gracious voice,
Have fixed my roving heart.   Ps. 73:25

Now, Lord, I would be Thine alone,
And wholly live to Thee;
But may I hope that Thou wilt own
A worthless worm, like me?

Yes! Though of sinners I'm the worst,   1 Tim. 2:15
I cannot doubt Thy will;
For if Thou hadst not loved me first
I had refused Thee still.   1 John 4:19

JOHN NEWTON

Reflection Questions:

1. Look at the second stanza: What sparked the transformation of the speaker of the hymn?

2. Reread the third stanza. Explain the image of the sun and the stars. How is the effect of coming to know Jesus like the sun rising in the morning?

3. The second to last stanza asks a question. What is the question? How does the final stanza answer the question?

59 – From Duty to Choice

Reading: Galatians 4:1-7

No strength of nature can suffice	
To serve the Lord aright;	
And what she has, she misapplies,	
For want of clearer light.	Rom. 7:15

How long beneath the Law I lay	Rom. 7:6, Gal. 3:23
In bondage and distress!	
I toiled the precept to obey,	
But toiled without success.	Rom. 7:23

Then to abstain from outward sin	
Was more than I could do;	
Now, if I feel its power within,	
I feel I hate it too.	Gal. 5:17

Then all my servile works were done	
A righteousness to raise;	Phil. 3:7-9
Now, freely chosen in the Son,	
I freely choose His ways.	

What shall I do was then the word,	
That I may worthier grow?	
What shall I render to the Lord?	Ps. 116:12
Is my inquiry now.	

To see the Law by Christ fulfilled,	Rom. 10:4
And hear His pardoning voice;	Gal. 3:24
Changes a slave into a child,	Gal. 4:7
And duty into choice.	Gal. 5:1

William Cowper

Reflection Questions:

1. How does the redemptive work of Christ free us up to serve God? In other words, how are the motives under grace different from those under law?

2. What does it mean to be changed from a slave to a child? How are the attitudes and motives of a child different from those of a servant?

3. Do you think there is a time and place for a sense of 'duty' to motivate Christian obedience? If so, when?

60 – The Debt of Gratitude

Reading: Psalm 126

When this passing world is done,   2 Pet. 3:12-13
When has sunk yon glaring sun,
When we stand with Christ on high
Looking o'er life's history,
Then, Lord, shall I fully know,
Not till then, how much I owe.

When I hear the wicked call
On the rocks and hills to fall,   Isa. 2:10, Rev. 6:16
When I see them start and shrink
On the fiery deluge brink,   Rev. 20:10
Then, Lord, shall I fully know,
Not till then, how much I owe.

When I stand before the throne,
Dressed in beauty not my own,   Isa. 61:10, Rev. 19:8
When I see thee as thou art,   1 John 3:2
Love thee with unsinning heart,
Then, Lord, shall I fully know,
Not till then, how much I owe.

When the praise of heav'n I hear,
Loud as thunders to the ear,   Rev. 19:6
Loud as many waters' noise,
Sweet as harp's melodious voice,
Then, Lord, shall I fully know,
Not till then, how much I owe.

Chosen not for good in me,	Deut. 7:7-8, Eph. 1:4
Wakened up from wrath to flee,	1 Thess. 1:10
Hidden in the Savior's side,	
By the Spirit sanctified,	1 Pet. 1:3
Teach me, Lord, on earth to show,	
By my love, how much I owe.	

ROBERT MURRAY M'CHENYE

Reflection Questions:

1. Why do we struggle to appreciate how much we 'owe' God?

2. Each stanza provides an imaginative point of view so that we can better appreciate our debt of gratitude to God. Which stanza do you think is most provocative and humbling?

3. Reflect on the last two lines of the hymn. What is the difference between love and gratitude? How are they related?

61 – The Joy of Indebtedness

Reading: Psalm 116:1-14

For mercies, countless as the sands   139:17-18
Which daily I receive
From Jesus, my Redeemer's hands,
My soul, what canst thou give?

Alas! from such a heart as mine,
What can I bring Him forth?   Ps. 116:12
My best is stained and dyed with sin,   Isa. 64:6, Zech. 3:3
My all is nothing worth.

Yet this acknowledgement I'll make
For all He has bestowed;
Salvation's sacred cup I'll take,
And call upon my God.   Ps. 116:13

The best return for one like me,
So wretched and so poor;
Is from His gifts to draw a plea,
And ask Him still for more.   Matt. 18:4

I cannot serve Him as I ought,
No works have I to boast;
Yet would I glory in the thought   1 Cor. 1:31, Jer. 9:23-24
That I shall owe Him most.

JOHN NEWTON

Reflection Questions:

1. Why is it so hard for us to accept that we cannot give anything to God?

2. Why is our 'best return' to 'ask Him still for more' (see the fourth stanza)?

3. Ponder the last two lines of the hymn. Try to put them into your own words. What is the hymn saying?

62 – Ten Thousand Reasons to Be Grateful

Reading: Psalm 103:1-5

When all thy Mercies, O my God,
My rising Soul surveys,
Why my cold Heart, art thou not lost
In Wonder, Love and Praise?

Thy Providence my Life sustain'd,
And all my Wants redrest,
When in the silent Womb I lay,   Ps. 139:13
And hung upon the breast.   Ps. 71:5-6

To all my weak Complaints and Cries
Thy Mercy lent an Ear,   Ps. 145:9
E'er yet my feeble Thoughts had learn'd
To form themselves in Prayer.   Ps 22:9

Unnumber'd Comforts on my Soul
Thy tender Care bestow'd,   Ps. 40:5
Before my infant Heart conceived
From whom those Comforts flow'd.

When in the slippery Paths of Youth   Ps. 25:7
With heedless Steps I ran,
Thine Arm unseen convey'd me safe,
And led me up to Man.   Ps. 23:3

Thro' hidden Dangers, Toils and Deaths
It gently clear'd my way;   Ps. 34:7
And thro' the pleasing Snares of Vice,
More to be fear'd than they.

Ten thousand thousand precious Gifts
My daily Thanks employ;   Ps. 34:1
Nor is the least a cheerful Heart,
That tastes these Gifts with Joy.   Ps. 34:8

Thro' every Period of my Life
Thy Goodness I'll pursue,   Ps. 23:6
And after Death in distant Worlds,
The pleasing Theme renew.

Thro' all Eternity to thee
A grateful Song I'll raise;
But o! Eternity's too short
To utter all thy Praise.[1]   Ps. 145:3

JOSEPH ADDISON

Reflection Questions:

1. Look at the first stanza. It mentions 'wonder, love, and praise.' How does thinking about God's goodness trigger these responses? Consider each in particular.

2. Psalm 103:2 calls us to be mindful of the blessings of the Lord. How does this hymn heighten our consciousness of God's abiding goodness?

3. Think back on the story of your life. How have you seen God clear a way for you through 'hidden dangers, toils, and deaths'?

---

1   Another hymn that describes a life saturated with praise is Horatius Bonar's 'Fill Thou my life, O Lord My God.'

63 – Submission

Reading: Genesis 32:22-32

Make me a captive, Lord,
And then I shall be free;   John 8:32
Force me to render up my sword,
And I shall conqueror be.   Rom. 8:37
I sink in life's alarms   Matt. 14:30
When by myself I stand;
Imprison me within thine arms,
And strong shall be my hand.   Neh. 6:9

My heart is weak and poor
Until it master find;
It has no spring of action sure,
It varies with the wind.   James 1:6
It cannot freely move
Till thou hast wrought its chain;
Enslave it with thy matchless love,
And deathless it shall reign.   Rom. 5:17

My power is faint and low
Till I have learned to serve;
It lacks the needed fire to glow,
It lacks the breeze to nerve;[1]
It cannot drive the world
Until itself be driven;
Its flag can only be unfurled
When thou shalt breathe from heaven.

---

1   'To nerve' here means to brace oneself for a difficult situation.

My will is not my own	
Till thou hast made it thine;	Luke 22:42
If it would reach a monarch's throne,	
It must its crown resign;	Mark 10:44
It only stands unbent	
Amid the clashing strife,	
When on thy bosom it has leant,	John 13:23
And found in thee its life.	John 1:4

GEORGE MATHESON

Reflection Questions:

1. A paradox is a statement that sounds contradictory, but in fact expresses a truth. How many paradoxical statements can you find in this hymn?

2. What does it mean that the will cannot be free until it has been taken captive by God? How are submission and freedom related?

3. Summarize the message of this hymn in one sentence.

64 – Yielding

Reading: Psalm 25:1-5

O Love that will not let me go, Rom. 8:35
I rest my weary soul in thee. Matt. 11:28
I give thee back the life I owe,
that in thine ocean depths its flow
may richer, fuller be.

O Light that follows all my way,
I yield my flick'ring torch to thee.
My heart restores its borrowed ray,
that in thy sunshine's blaze its day
may brighter, fairer be.

O Joy that seekest me through pain,
I cannot close my heart to thee.
I trace the rainbow through the rain,
and feel the promise is not vain,
that morn shall tearless be. Ps. 30:5

O Cross that liftest up my head, Ps. 3:3
I dare not ask to fly from thee.
I lay in dust, life's glory dead,
and from the ground there blossoms red,
life that shall endless be.

GEORGE MATHESON

Reflection Questions:

1. What does it mean to yield our lives to God? How does this hymn depict such yielding?

2. What is the effect of yielding our lives to God? Look at the last two lines of stanza one and two for insight.

3. Ponder the final lines of the hymn. The color red is striking. Why is this color mentioned? What is the connection between this color and endless life?

65 – Obedience

Reading: Luke 14:25-33

Jesus calls us o'er the tumult
Of our life's wild, restless sea;
Day by day his sweet voice soundeth,
Saying, "Christian, follow me." Mark 1:17

As, of old, apostles heard it
By the Galilean lake,
Turned from home and toil and kindred,
Leaving all for his dear sake. Mark 1:18

Jesus calls us from the worship
Of the vain world's golden store,
From each idol that would keep us,
Saying, "Christian, love me more."

In our joys and in our sorrows,
Days of toil and hours of ease,
Still he calls, in cares and pleasures, Luke 8:14
"Christian, love me more than these."

Jesus calls us: by thy mercies, Rom. 12:1
Savior, may we hear thy call,
Give our hearts to thine obedience, John 14:21
Serve and love thee best of all.[1] Luke 14:26, 33

CECIL FRANCES ALEXANDER

---

1   Another great hymn on obedience is 'When We Cannot See Our Way' by Thomas Kelly.

Reflection Questions:

1. What is the relationship between obedience and love?

2. What does it mean to answer the call, 'Christian, love me more?'

3. What are the idols in your life that impede your freedom to serve Christ wholeheartedly?

66 – Self-Denial

Reading: Luke 9:23-26

Jesus, I my cross have taken,   Luke 14:27
All to leave and follow Thee.
Destitute, despised, forsaken,   Isa. 53:3
Thou from hence my all shall be.
Perish every fond ambition,
All I've sought or hoped or known.
Yet how rich is my condition!   Ps. 16:5-6
God and Heaven are still mine own.

Let the world despise and leave me,
They have left my Savior, too.   Heb. 13:13
Human hearts and looks deceive me;
Thou art not, like them, untrue.   Num. 23:19
And while Thou shalt smile upon me,
God of wisdom, love and might,
Foes may hate and friends disown me,
Show Thy face and all is bright.

Go, then, earthly fame and treasure!
Come, disaster, scorn and pain!
In Thy service, pain is pleasure;
With Thy favor, loss is gain.   Phil. 3:8
I have called Thee, Abba, Father;   Rom. 8:15
I have set my heart on Thee:
Storms may howl, and clouds may gather,
All must work for good to me.   Rom. 8:28

Man may trouble and distress me,
'Twill but drive me to Thy breast.
Life with trials hard may press me;   2 Cor. 4:8
Heaven will bring me sweeter rest.   Rev. 14:13
Oh, 'tis not in grief to harm me
While Thy love is left to me;
Oh, 'twere not in joy to charm me,
Were that joy unmixed with Thee.

Take, my soul, thy full salvation;   Ps. 116:13
Rise o'er sin, and fear, and care;
Joy to find in every station
Something still to do or bear:
Think what Spirit dwells within thee;   Rom. 8:11
What a Father's smile is thine;   Rom. 8:32
What a Savior died to win thee,   Rom. 8:34
Child of heaven, shouldst thou repine?

Haste then on from grace to glory,
Armed by faith, and winged by prayer,
Heaven's eternal day's before thee,   Heb. 4:9
God's own hand shall guide thee there.
Soon shall close thy earthly mission,
Swift shall pass thy pilgrim days;
Hope soon change to glad fruition,
Faith to sight, and prayer to praise.   1 Cor. 13:12

HENRY FRANCIS LYTE

Reflection Questions:

1. How does this hymn help us to understand what it means to fulfill Luke 9:23?

2. How does the hymn show the relationship between the difficulty of discipleship and the joy of discipleship?

3. Reread the final line. What does it mean for faith to become sight and for prayer to become praise?

67 – *Humility*

Reading: Matthew 18:1-5

As helpless as a child who clings,
Fast to his father's arm,
And casts his weakness on the strength   1 Pet. 5:6-7
That keeps him safe from harm;
So I, my Father, cling to Thee,
And every passing hour
Would link my earthly feebleness
To Thine Almighty power.

As trustful as a child who looks
Up in his mother's face,
And all his little griefs and fears
Forgets in her embrace;   Isa. 49:15
So I to Thee, my Savior, look
And in Thy face Divine,
Can read the love that will sustain
As weak a faith as mine.

As loving as a child who sits
Close by his parent's knee,   Isa. 66:12-13
And knows no want while it can have
That sweet society;
So, sitting at Thy feet, my heart
Would all its love outpour,   Luke 7:38
And pray that Thou wouldst teach
    me, Lord,
To love Thee more and more.

JAMES DRUMMOND BURNS

Reflection Questions:

1. Read the first line of each stanza. What three traits of children does the hymn use to describe the attitude of faith?

2. The hymn depicts both the relationship of a child with his father and with his mother. How does the relationship between a father and a child help us to understand the love of God? How does the relationship between a mother and child help us to understand the love of God?

3. What barriers keep you from having a childlike faith in God?

68 – Trust

Reading: Psalm 131

> *Thy way, not mine, O Lord,*
> *However dark it be;*   Ps. 23:4
> *Lead me by Thine own hand,*   Ps. 139:10
> *Choose out the Path for me.*
>
> *Smooth let it be, or rough,*
> *It will be still the best;*
> *Winding or straight it leads*
> *Right onward to Thy rest.*   Matt. 11:28-30
>
> *I dare not choose my lot;*
> *I would not if I might:*
> *Choose Thou for me, my God,*
> *So shall I walk aright.*
>
> *Take Thou my cup, and it*   Ps. 116:13
> *With joy or sorrow fill,*
> *As best to Thee may seem;*
> *Choose Thou my good and ill.*
>
> *Choose Thou for me my friends,*
> *My sickness or my health.*
> *Choose Thou my cares for me,*
> *My poverty or wealth.*   Phil. 4:11-13
>
> *Not mine, not mine the choice,*   Luke 22:42
> *In things both great and small;*
> *Be Thou my guide, my strength,*
> *My wisdom and my all.*[1]

HORATIUS BONAR

---

1   Another hymn that is helpful to read alongside this one is James Montgomery's 'One Prayer I Have, All Prayers in One'. For insight into the particular sins that threaten faith, see the final stanza of William Cowper's 'By Whom Was David Taught'.

Reflection Questions:

1. How does this hymn help us to pray the words of Jesus, 'Not my will, but yours be done' (Luke 22:42)?

2. Why do we find it so difficult to trust God absolutely with all details of our lives?

3. Are you willing to pray the words of this hymn to God? If the answer is 'no', what is holding you back?

69 – *Fortitude*

Reading: 2 Corinthians 4:7-11

Workman of God! O lose not heart,
But learn what God is like;
And in the darkest battlefield
Thou shalt know where to strike.

Thrice blest is he to whom is giv'n
The instinct that can tell
That God is on the field, when He
Is most invisible.   2 Kings 6:16

Blest too is he who can divine
Where real right doth lie,
And dares to take the side that seems
Wrong to man's blindfold eye.   Acts 5:29

Then learn to scorn the praise of men,
And learn to lose with God;
For Jesus won the world through shame,   Heb. 12:2-3
And beckons thee His road.

For right is right, since God is God,
And right the day must win;
To doubt would be disloyalty,
To falter would be sin.   Luke 9:62

FREDERICK FABER

Reflection Questions:

1. What 'instinct' is mentioned in the second stanza? How do you develop this ability?

2. What does it mean to 'learn to lose with God?' This is a strange phrase. How does the line that follows this phrase help to clarify the meaning?

3. Explain the final two lines of the hymn. How do they fit into the hymn as a whole?

70 – Hope

Reading: Romans 4:13-25

Father of Jesus Christ, my Lord,	
My Saviour, and my Head,	
I trust in Thee, whose powerful word	
Hath raised Him from the dead.	Rom. 4:24

Eternal life to all mankind	John 3:16
Thou hast in Jesus given;	
And all who seek, in Him shall find	Matt. 7:7
The happiness of heaven.	

Faith in Thy power Thou seest I have,	
For Thou this faith has wrought;	Eph. 2:8
Dead souls Thou callest from their grave,	
And speakest worlds from nought.	Rom. 4:17

In hope, against all human hope,	Rom. 4:18
Self-desperate, I believe;	
Thy quickening word shall raise me up,	
Thou shalt Thy Spirit give.	Rom. 5:5

Faith, mighty faith, the promise sees,	
And looks to that alone;	Rom. 4:20
Laughs at impossibilities,	
And cries: It shall be done!	Rom. 4:21

CHARLES WESLEY

Reflection Questions:

1. How are faith and hope related? What is the difference between them?

2. Explain the meaning of the following line: 'Self-desperate, I believe?' What does it mean to be self-desperate?

3. Reread the final stanza. What does it mean to laugh at impossibilities? What Old Testament stories does this idea bring to remembrance?

71 – *Courage*

Reading: Revelation 14:1-5

Am I a soldier of the cross?	1 Tim. 2:4
A follower of the Lamb?	Rev. 14:4
And shall I fear to own his cause?	
Or blush to speak his name?	Rom. 1:16

Must I be carry'd to the skies
On flowery beds of ease,
While others fought to win the prize, 1 Cor. 9:24
And sail'd through bloody seas?

Are there no foes for me to face?
Must I not stem the flood?
Is this vile world a friend to grace,
To help me on to GOD?

Sure I must fight if I would reign; 2 Tim. 2:12
Increase my courage LORD:
I'll bear the cross, endure the pain, Luke 9:23
Supported by thy word.

Thy saints, in all this glorious war,
Shall conquer though they die; Rev. 12:11
They see the triumph from afar,
And seize it with their eye.

When that illustrious day shall rise,
And all thy armies shine,
In robes of vic'try through the skies, Rev. 7:14
The glory shall be thine.

Isaac Watts

Reflection Questions:

1. What is your reaction to the second stanza of the hymn?

2. Why is courage a necessary virtue for the Christian life?

3. The book of Revelation speaks often of Christians conquering through their endurance. What does it mean to conquer as a Christian (Rev. 2:7, 2:11, 2:17, etc.)?

72 – *Godly Fear*

Reading: Psalm 119:1-8

I want a principle within
Of jealous godly fear,   Heb. 12:28
A sensibility of sin,
A pain to feel it near.

I want the first approach to feel
Of pride, or fond desire;
To catch the wandering of my will,   Ps. 119:36-37
And quench the kindling fire.

That I from thee no more may part,
No more thy goodness grieve,   Eph. 4:30
The filial awe, the fleshly heart,   1 Pet. 1:17, Ezek. 36:26
The tender conscience give.   1 Tim. 1:5

Quick as the apple of an eye,
O God, my conscience make;
Awake my soul, when sin is nigh,   1 Cor. 15:34
And keep it still awake.   Rom. 13:11-14

If to the right or left I stray,
That moment, Lord, reprove;   Isa. 30:21
And let me weep my life away,   Matt. 5:4
For having griev'd thy love.

O may the least omission pain
My well-instructed soul,   Ps. 19:14
And drive me to the blood again,
Which makes the wounded whole.

CHARLES WESLEY

Reflection Questions:

1. This hymn describes the keystone traits of a tender conscience. Why is it important to have a conscience that is sensitive to the movements of sin?

2. What traits of a tender conscience are lacking in your own character?

3. Why does the hymn end with a reference to the cleansing power of the blood of Jesus?

73 – Joy

Reading: John 15:11

Come ye that love the Lord,
And let your Joys be known,
Join in a Song with sweet accord,
While ye surround the Throne.   Rev. 14:3

The sorrows of the mind,
Be banished from this place;
Religion never was design'd;
To make our pleasures less.

Let those refuse to sing
That never knew our God;
But Servants of the heavenly King
May speak their Joys abroad.

The God that rules on high,
That all the Earth surveys
That rides upon the stormy Sky,   Ps. 104:3
And calms the roaring Seas.   Mark 4:39

This awful God is ours,
Our Father and our Love: Matt. 6:9
Thou shalt send down his
   heavenly Powers
To carry us above.

There we shall see thy Face,   Matt. 5:8
And never, never Sin;
There from the Rivers of thy Grace,
Drink endless Pleasures in.   Ps. 36:8

Yes, and before we rise
To that immortal State,
The Thoughts of such amazing Bliss,
Shou'd constant Joys create.

The Men of Grace have found
Glory begun below;
Celestial Fruits on earthly Ground
From Faith and Hope may grow.

The hill of Zion yields
A thousand sacred sweets,
Before we reach the heavenly fields,
Or walk the golden streets.   Rev. 21:21

Then let our Songs abound,
And every Tear be dry;   Rev. 21:4
We're marching thro' Immanuel's
*   Ground*
To fairer Worlds on high.

ISAAC WATTS

Reflection Questions:

1. What is your reaction to the second stanza of the hymn? Why would this stanza surprise a lot of non-Christians?

2. What do the following lines mean: 'Celestial Fruits on earthly Ground/From Faith and Hope may grow?' In what sense do we get foretastes of heaven on earth?

3. According to this hymn, what is the source of the unique joy that Christians experience in this life?

5

MEDITATING ON SPIRITUAL DISCIPLINES

Imagine watching a tourist who is bumbling through the streets of Rome. You can see that he is being sidetracked by every huckster on the curbside who is trying to convince him that an authentic experience of the city can be purchased at the price of a toy replica of the Colosseum and a burnt slice of pizza. Clearly, no forethought has gone into planning this trip. So, you pull him aside and ask him if he has ever heard of St. Peter's Basilica. He hasn't. Restraining your surprise, you graciously take a couple of minutes to describe to him what, for many, is a sight sufficiently beautiful to be mistaken for the antechamber of heaven. You tell him about Bernini's Canopy, Michelangelo's Pieta, the Dome, and so on and so forth. By the time you finish your description you can see clearly that the man's appetite for pizza has all but evaporated.

But the conversation does not end with the mere whetting of an appetite. Now that interest has been piqued, a further step must be taken: you must make sure that the tourist can find his way to the desired destination. And so, you hand the man a map of Rome, locate the basilica on the map, draw a big circle around the location, and then trace a path through the streets for him to follow. Only after all of this is finished, is the tourist ready to be sent off on his way to go and experience something far more memorable and satisfying than a cheap lunch.

This image explains the purpose of this next set of hymns. The hope of the first three groups was to stir the heart to desire something more than the plastic trinkets of the world. Holiness, the gospel, communion with God, and growth in virtue – these are incomparable goods on offer for human beings to taste and enjoy. The main purpose of everything done thus far is to feed a surging hunger to go out and experience more of the abundant life that is made available exclusively through Jesus Christ (c.f. John 10:10).

Now, once spiritual appetites are awakened, the next step to be taken is to map an itinerary that will show eager Christians how to draw closer to God. Spiritual disciplines are the landmarks of this itinerary. They are the surest path to godliness. By habitually reading our Bibles, making time for prayer, repenting, and practicing other disciplines, we plod our way to the purity of heart, which Jesus tells us is the precondition of seeing God (Matthew 5:3).

Once again, relevance, not thoroughness, has been our guide in selecting these hymns. No attempt has been made to provide a comprehensive landscape of the spiritual disciplines. Just as a good fitness instructor chooses workouts based on the needs of his clients, the hymns in this section have been chosen because they address weaknesses of modern Christians. In fact, the analogy can be pressed further. It is not uncommon for someone working out with a trainer to be confused by the usefulness of an exercise. Yet, good coaches know what they are doing. Stretching and building muscle may not appear to be connected. But anyone with hamstring problems will appreciate the difficulty of doing heavy deadlifts with a pulled muscle.

Something similar is true of the following hymns. Some may seem less relevant than others. However, do not be deceived by a first reading. Each hymn has been included because it touches some spiritual muscle that is in desperate need of being stretched or toned. Remember: the recipe for fitness is never 'do what's easy' or 'stick to what feels comfortable.' Fitness is a product of discomfort. Keep this in mind as you complete the next set of exercises.

THE DISCIPLINE OF BIBLE READING

74 – The Spirit Must Illumine the Word

Reading: 1 Corinthians 2:10-16

Come, Holy Ghost, our hearts inspire;	
Let us thine influence prove;	
Source of the old prophetic fire,	1 Pet. 1:10-11
Fountain of life and love.	John 7:37-39
Come, Holy Ghost, for moved by thee	
The prophets wrote and spoke:	2 Pet. 1:20-21
Unlock the truth, thyself the key;	John 14:26
Unseal the sacred book.	1 Cor. 2:14-16
Expand thy wings, Celestial Dove;	Matt. 3:16
Brood o'er our nature's night;	Gen. 1:3
On our disordered spirits move,	
And let there now be light.	2 Cor. 3:16
God, through himself, we then shall know,	1 Cor. 2:10-13
If thou within us shine;	
And sound, with all thy saints below,	
The depths of love divine.	Eph. 3:10-16

CHARLES WESLEY

Reflection Questions:

1. Why do we need the Holy Spirit in order to read the Word of God?

2. How is Genesis 1:3 a helpful picture for thinking about the role of the Spirit in helping us to read the Word of God?

3. Reread the final stanza. What does it mean, 'God, through himself, we then shall know'? How does this stanza help us to understand 1 Corinthians 2:11-12?

75 – *The Sanctifying Light of the Word*

Reading: Psalm 19:7-14

The Spirit breathes upon the word,	2 Tim. 3:16
And brings the truth to sight;	Ps. 119:18
Precepts and promises afford	
A sanctifying light.	Ps. 19:8
A glory gilds the sacred page,	
Majestic, like the sun;	Ps. 19:4-6
It gives a light to every age;	
It gives, but borrows none.	2 Pet. 1:19
The hand that gave it still supplies	
The gracious light and heat;	Mal. 4:2
Its truths upon the nations rise;--	
They rise, but never set.	
Let everlasting thanks be thine,	
For such a bright display	Ps. 36:9
As makes a world of darkness shine	
With beams of heavenly day.	Isa. 30:26
My soul rejoices to pursue	
The steps of him I love,	John 8:12
Till glory breaks upon my view,	
In brighter worlds above.	Rev. 21:22-23

WILLIAM COWPER

Reflection Questions:

1. According to the first stanza, what does the Spirit do for the word of God?

2. The third stanza speaks of God as supplying light and heat through His Word. Why do we need light when we read the Scriptures? Why do we need heat?

3. How does this hymn help us to understand the meaning of John 8:12?

76 – The Word Gives Us Life

Reading: 2 Timothy 3:14-17

Laden with Guilt, and full of Fears,
I fly to Thee, my Lord,
And not a Glimpse of Hope appears,
But in thy written Word.

The Volume of my Father's Grace
Does all my Griefs assuage;
Here I behold my Saviour's Face
Almost in ev'ry Page.   Luke 24:27

This is the Field where hidden lies
The Pearl of Price unknown;   Matt. 13:44-46
That Merchant is divinely wise,
Who makes the Pearl his own.

Here consecrated Water flows,
To quench my Thirst of Sin;   John 7:37-38
Here the fair Tree of Knowledge grows,   Gen 2:17, Prov. 3:18
No Danger dwells therein.   Prov. 30:5

This is the Judge that ends the Strife
Where Wit and Reason fail:
My Guide to everlasting Life,   John 6:68
Through all this gloomy Vale.

O may thy Counsels, mighty God,
My roving Feet command,   Ps. 119:67
Nor I forsake the happy Road
That leads to thy Right Hand.   Ps. 16:11

Isaac Watts

Reflection Questions:

1. What is the condition of the speaker before he begins to read the Scriptures?

2. What is unique about the word of God according to the hymn? What does it offer that cannot be found anywhere else?

3. Consider the following lines: 'Here I behold my Saviour's Face/Almost in ev'ry Page?' How do we learn to see the face of Jesus, not only in the New Testament, but also in the Old Testament?

77 – *Meditating on the Word Day and Night*

Reading: Psalm 1

When quiet in my house I sit,
Thy book be my companion still;
My joy Thy sayings to repeat,
Talk o'er the records of Thy will,
And search the oracles divine,
Till every heart-felt word be mine.

O may the gracious words divine
Subject of all my converse[1] be!
So will the Lord His follower join, Luke 24:15
And walk and talk Himself with me;
So shall my heart His presence prove,
And burn with everlasting love. Luke 24:32

Oft as I lay me down to rest,
O may the reconciling word 2 Cor. 5:19
Sweetly compose my weary breast!
While, on the bosom of my Lord, John 13:23
I sink in blissful dreams away, Ps. 3:5, 4:8
And visions of eternal day. Rev. 22:5

Rising to sing my Savior's praise,
Thee may I publish all day long;
And let Thy precious word of grace Acts 20:32
Flow from my heart, and fill my
 tongue;
Fill all my life with purest love,
And join me to the church above.

Charles Wesley

---

1 Conversation

Reflection Questions:

1. How does the line 'Till every heart-felt word is mine' reveal the goal of meditating on the Word?

2. Reread the second stanza. What is the gift that often comes through meditating on the word of God?

3. According to the third stanza, what benefit comes from meditating on the Word before going to sleep?

THE DISCIPLINE OF PRAYER

78 – *The Essence of Prayer*

Reading: Matthew 6:5-8

Prayer is the soul's sincere desire
Uttered or unexpressed;
The motion of a hidden fire
That trembles in the breast.

Prayer is the burden of a sigh,
The falling of a tear;
The upward glancing of an eye,
When none but God is near.   Ps. 73:25-26

Prayer is the simplest form of speech
That infant lips can try;   Ps. 8:2
Prayer the sublimest strains that
     reach
The Majesty on high.

Prayer is the contrite sinner's voice,
Returning from his ways,
While angels in their songs rejoice,
And cry, "Behold he prays!"   Luke 15:10

Prayer is the Christian's vital breath,
The Christian's native air;
His watchword at the gates of death,–
He enters heaven with prayer.

The saints, in prayer, appear as one
In word, and deed, and mind;
While with the Father and the Son
Sweet fellowship they find.   1 John 1:3

Nor prayer is made by man alone;
The Holy Spirit pleads;   Rom 8:26
And Jesus, on the eternal throne
For sinners intercedes.   Rom 8:34

Thou by Whom we come to God,
The Life, the Truth, the Way,   John 14:6
The path of prayer Thyself hast trod;
Lord, teach us how to pray.   Luke 11:1

JAMES MONTGOMERY

Reflection Questions:

1. The hymn answers the question, 'What is prayer?' Do you find anything surprising about the answer given in the hymn?

2. What does it mean that 'Prayer is the Christian's vital breath/The Christian's native air?' How is prayer like breath and air?

3. If someone asked you the question, 'What is prayer?' how would you answer?

79 – Stop Complaining; Start Praying

Reading: Psalm 81:8-16

What various hindrances we meet
In coming to a mercy seat?
Yet who that knows the worth of prayer,
But wishes to be often there.

Prayer makes the darkened cloud withdraw,
Prayer climbs the ladder Jacob saw;   Gen. 28:10-17
Gives exercise to faith and love,
Brings every blessing from above.   Luke 11:9

Restraining prayer, we cease to fight;   Matt. 26:41
Prayer makes the Christian's armor bright;   Eph. 6:18
And Satan trembles, when he sees
The weakest saint upon his knees.

While Moses stood with arms spread wide,
Success was found on Israel's side;
But when thro' weariness they failed,
That moment Amalek prevailed.   Exod. 17:11

Have you no words? Ah, think again,
Words flow apace when you complain;   Exod. 17:3
And fill your fellow creature's ear
With the sad tale of all your care.

Were half the breath thus vainly spent,
To Heav'n in supplication sent;
Your cheerful song would oftener be,
Hear what the Lord has done for me![1]   Ps. 66:16

WILLIAM COWPER

---

1   For all of the spiritual benefits of prayer, see 'Pray'r Was Appointed to Convey' by Joseph Hart.

Reflection Questions:

1. What does it mean, 'Restraining prayer, we cease to fight?' How is prayer a form of warfare?

2. Why does Satan tremble when he sees 'the weakest saint upon his knees?'

3. What is your reaction to the final stanza? How can we learn to complain less and pray more?

80 – Prayer Is Warfare

Reading: Luke 22:39-46

To keep your armour bright,	Eph. 6:11
Attend with constant care,	
Still walking in your Captain's sight,	Heb. 2:10
And watching unto prayer.	Matt. 26:41
Ready for all alarms,	
Steadfastly set your face,	Isa. 50:7
And always exercise your arms,	
And use your every grace.	
Pray, without ceasing, pray,	1 Thess. 5:17
Your Captain gives the word;	
His summons cheerfully obey,	
And call upon the Lord:	Ps. 50:15
To God your every want	
In instant prayer display;	Neh. 2:4
Pray always; pray, and never faint;	Eph. 6:18, Luke 21:36
Pray, without ceasing pray!	
In fellowship, alone,	Luke 4:42
To God with faith draw near,	Heb. 4:16-18
Approach His courts, besiege His throne	Luke 18:1-8
With all the powers of prayer:	
Go to His temple, go,	
Nor from His altar move;	Luke 2:37
Let every house His worship know,	
And every heart His love.	
To God your spirits dart;	Neh. 2:4
Your souls in words declare;	
Or groan, to Him who reads the heart,	Rom. 8:27
The unutterable prayer:	Rom. 8:26
His mercy now implore,	
And now show forth His praise;	Isa. 43:21
In shouts, or silent awe, adore	
His miracles of grace.	

Pour out your souls to God,	Ps. 62:8
And bow them with your knees,	
And spread your hearts and	
hands abroad,	1 Tim. 2:8
And pray for Zion's peace;	Ps. 122:6-9
Your guides and brethren bear	
For ever on your mind:	Eph. 1:16
Extend the arms of mighty prayer,	
In grasping all mankind.	1 Tim. 2:1

From strength to strength go on,	Ps. 84:7
Wrestle, and fight, and pray,	Col. 4:12
Tread all the powers of darkness	
down,	Luke 10:19
And win the well-fought day;	1 Tim. 6:12, 2 Tim. 4:6-7
Still let the Spirit cry	
In all His soldiers: Come!	Rev. 22:17
Till Christ the Lord descend	
from high,	
And take the conquerors home.[1]	Rom. 8:37

CHARLES WESLEY

Reflection Questions:

1. How does prayer keep our 'armour bright?'

2. What does it mean 'to besiege' the throne of God with prayer?

3. Reread the final stanza. Why is wrestling a helpful image for thinking about the difficulty of prayer? How does this hymn help us find the motivation we need to persevere in prayer?

---

1 Three other hymns to challenge your heart regarding prayer are 'Jesu, Thou Sovereign Lord of All' and 'Jesus, My Strength, My Hope' by Charles Wesley and 'I Bring My Heart to Thee' by Francis Havergal.

THE DISCIPLINE OF REPENTANCE AND MORTIFICATION

81 – *The Longing for Nearness to God*

Readings: Isaiah 59:1-2, Psalm 42:1-5

O for a closer walk with God,
A calm and heav'nly frame,
A light to shine upon the road
That leads me to the Lamb!

Where is the blessedness I knew
When first I sought the Lord?   Ps. 51:12
Where is the soul refreshing view   Acts 3:19-20
Of Jesus and His Word?

What peaceful hours I then enjoyed!
How sweet their mem'ry still!   Ps. 42:4
But they have left an aching void
The world can never fill.

Return, O holy Dove, return,   Ps. 51:11
Sweet messenger of rest;
I hate the sins that made Thee mourn,   Eph. 4:30
And drove Thee from my breast.

The dearest idol I have known,
Whate'er that idol be,
Help me to tear it from Thy throne
And worship only Thee.

So shall my walk be close with God,
Calm and serene my frame;
So purer light shall mark the road
That leads me to the Lamb.

WILLIAM COWPER

Reflection Questions:

1. Why does sin leave us feeling 'an aching void'?

2. The fourth stanza can be confusing. How does Ephesians 4:30 help us to understand what the hymn writer is saying?

3. The hymn speaks of the need 'to tear' idols from the heart. How do we go about doing this? How do we get rid of something that has hijacked our worship?

82 – *The Gift of a Broken Heart*

Reading: 2 Corinthians 7:8-11

Savior, Prince of Israel's race,	Isa. 9:6
See me from Thy lofty throne;	
Give the sweet relenting grace,	
Soften this obdurate stone!	
Stone to flesh, O God, convert;	Ezek. 36:26
Cast a look, and break my heart!	
By Thy Spirit, Lord, reprove,	
All my inmost sins reveal,	Ps. 139:23-24
Sins against Thy light and love	
Let me see, and let me feel;	
Sins that crucified my God,	
Spilt again Thy precious blood.	Heb. 6:6
Jesu, seek Thy wandering sheep,	Luke 15:3; Isa. 53:6
Make me restless to return;	
Bid me look on Thee, and weep,	Zech. 12:10
Bitterly as Peter mourn,	Luke 22:62
Till I say, by grace restored,	
Now Thou know'st I love Thee, Lord	John 21:17
Might I in Thy sight appear,	
As the publican distressed,	
Stand, not daring to draw near,	
Smite on my unworthy breast,	
Groan the sinner's only plea,	
God, be merciful to me!	Luke 18:13

O remember me for good,
Passing through the mortal vale!
Show me the atoning blood,   Col. 1:20
When my strength and spirit fail;
Give my gasping soul to see
Jesus crucified for me!

CHARLES WESLEY

Reflection Questions:

1. The first stanza asks for Jesus to break the heart of stone. Why do we sometimes need God to break our hearts?[1]

2. The second stanza asks not only to 'see' sin but to 'feel' sin. Why is feeling an important part of repentance (for help, see 2 Corinthians 7:10-11)?

3. The hymn refers to both sins against light and sins against love. What is the difference between these? Give an example of a sin against light. Give an example of a sin against love.

---

1   For another powerful hymn on this topic see 'Infinite Grief! Amazing Woe!' by Isaac Watts.

83 – Transparent Confession

Reading: Psalm 51:1-4

> *Not what these hands have done*
> *Can save this guilty soul;*   Rom. 3:20
> *Not what this toiling flesh has borne*
> *Can make my spirit whole.*

> *Not what I feel or do*
> *Can give me peace with God;*
> *Not all my prayers and sighs and tears*
> *Can bear my awful load.*   Ps. 38:4

> *Thy work alone, O Christ,*
> *Can ease this weight of sin;*   Rom. 3:22
> *Thy blood alone, O Lamb of God,*
> *Can give me peace within.*   Col. 1:20

> *Thy love to me, O God,*
> *Not mine, O Lord, to Thee,*   Ps. 51:1
> *Can rid me of this dark unrest,*
> *And set my spirit free.*

> *Thy grace alone, O God,*
> *To me can pardon speak;*   Ps. 32:1-2
> *Thy power alone, O Son of God,*
> *Can this sore bondage break.*

> *I bless the Christ of God;*
> *I rest on love Divine;*
> *And with unfaltering lip and heart,*
> *I call this Savior mine.*[1]

HORATIUS BONAR

---

1   Two other hymns that draw us into transparent confession are 'Just as I Am' by Charlotte Elliott and 'Out of My Bondage, Sorrow, and Night' by William Sleeper.

Reflection Questions:

1. The hymn starts with four statements that all begin with the word 'not'. What is the main idea of these statements?

2. The hymn speaks of the ability of Jesus to free us from both the guilt and power of sin. How does Jesus free us from the guilt of sin? How does He free us from the power of sin?

3. The final stanza uses the word 'unfaltering.' Why is this word significant? What is the difference between a faltering profession of faith and an unfaltering profession of faith?

84 – Christ, Our Sin Offering

Reading: Hebrews 9:23-28

Not all the blood of beasts
On Jewish altars slain,
Could give the guilty conscience
*   peace,*
Or wash away the stain.   Heb. 10:1-4

But Christ, the heav'nly Lamb,   John 1:29, Rev. 13:8
Takes all our sins away,   Heb. 10:12
A sacrifice of nobler name
And richer blood than they.   Heb. 9:22

My faith would lay her hand
On that dear head of thine,   Lev. 4:29
While like a penitent I stand,
And there confess my sin.   Lev. 16:21

My soul looks back to see
The burdens thou didst bear,   Lev. 16:22, Isa. 53:6
When hanging on the cursed tree,   Deut. 21:23, Gal. 3:13
And knows her guilt was there.

Believing, we rejoice
To see the curse remove;   John 19:30, Matt. 27:50-51
We bless the Lamb with
*   cheerful voice,*
And sing his bleeding love.   Rev. 5:9-10

ISAAC WATTS

Reflection Questions:

1. Why couldn't the 'blood of beasts' under the old covenant atone for the guilt of human sin (c.f. Heb. 10:4)?

2. What does it mean for 'faith' to 'lay her hand' on the head of Christ? If you are unsure, read Leviticus 4 and 16.

3. Read Hebrews 10:14. What is the comfort of this verse?

85 – The Passion for Purity

Reading: 1 John 1:5-10

Jesus, Thy boundless love to me,
no thought can reach, no tongue declare;
O knit my thankful heart to Thee,
and reign without a rival there.   Gal. 2:20
Thine wholly, Thine alone, I am;
be Thou my Rod and Staff and Guide.

O grant that nothing in my soul
may dwell, but Thy pure love alone!   Eph. 3:17
O may Thy love possess my whole,
my Joy, my Treasure, and my Crown.   Col. 2:3
All coldness from my heart remove;
my ev'ry act, word, thought, be love.

O love, how cheering is thy ray!
All pain before thy presence flies;
care, anguish, sorrow, melt away,
where'er thy healing beams arise.   Mal. 4:2
O Jesus, nothing may I see,
nothing desire or seek, but Thee.   Ps. 73:25

This love unwearied I pursue
and dauntlessly to Thee aspire.   Phil. 3:12-14
O may Thy love my hope renew,
burn in my soul like heav'nly fire.
And day and night, be all my care
to guard this sacred treasure there.[1]

PAUL GERHARDT *Trans.* JOHN WESLEY

---

1 Two similar hymns worth reading are 'Thou Hidden Love of God Whose Height' by Gerhard Tersteegen and 'Thee Will I Love' by Angelus Silesius. Both are translated by John Wesley.

Reflection Questions:

1. What does it mean for Christ to reign in our hearts without a rival?

2. The ultimate goal of repentance is not to turn away from sin, but to turn toward holiness. How does this hymn capture what it looks like to long for holiness?

3. The final stanza of the hymn pictures love as a burning fire. How is the image of having to guard a fire useful for thinking about what it looks like to maintain a pure heart for God?

THE DISCIPLINE OF PRACTICING THE PRESENCE OF GOD

86 – Practicing the Presence of God by Means of Creation

Reading: Psalm 104:24-30

There is a book, who runs may read,	
Which heavenly truth imparts;	Ps. 104:24
And all the lore its scholars need,	
Pure eyes and loving hearts.	Matt. 6:22
The works of God, above, below,	Ps. 111:2
Within us, and around,	
Are pages in that book, to show	
How God himself is found.	Ps. 19:1-4
The glorious sky, embracing all,	
Is like the Father's love;	Ps. 36:5
Wherewith encompassed, great and small	
In peace and order move.	
One Name above all glorious names,	Eph. 1:21
With its ten thousand tongues	
The everlasting sea proclaims,	Ps. 104:25
Echoing angelic songs.	Luke 2:14
The dew of heaven is like His grace;	
It steals in silence down;	Num. 11:9
But where it lights, the favored place	
By richest fruits is known.	

Two worlds are ours; 'tis only sin
Forbids us to descry[1]
The mystic heaven and earth within,   Luke 17:21
Plain as the earth and sky.

Thou, who hast given me eyes to see
And love this sight so fair,
Give me a heart to find out Thee,
And read Thee everywhere!   Ps. 139:7

JOHN KEBLE

Reflection Questions:

1. How is God's creation like a book that can be read with the eyes of faith?

2. Why are 'pure eyes' and a 'loving heart' needed to read the book of creation correctly?

3. We often think of science as revealing the secret coding of the universe. However, according to the final line of the hymn, what is the most profound truth that the universe reveals?

---

1   Catch sight of.

87 – Practicing the Presence of God in the Busyness of Life

Reading: Luke 10:38-42

Still with Thee, O my God,
I would desire to be;
By day, by night, at home, abroad,
I would be still with Thee.

With Thee when dawn comes in
And calls me back to care,
Each day returning to begin
With Thee, my God, in prayer.   Ps. 5:3

With Thee amid the crowd
That throngs the busy mart,[1]   Luke 10:39
To hear Thy voice, where time's is loud,
Speak softly to my heart.

With Thee when day is done,
And evening calms the mind;
The setting as the rising sun   Ps. 3:5
With Thee my heart would find.

With Thee when darkness brings
The signal of repose,
Calm in the shadow of Thy wings,   Ps. 91:1
Mine eyelids I would close.   Ps. 4:8

With Thee, in Thee, by faith
Abiding, I would be;   John 15:5
By day, by night, in life, in death,
I would be still with Thee.[2]

JAMES DRUMMOND BURNS

---

1 A busy marketplace.

2 Thomas Ken wrote two remarkable hymns, one for the start of each day and another for the end. They are 'Awake, My Soul, and with the Sun' and 'Glory to Thee, My God, This Night.'

Reflection Questions:

1. This hymn is about being attentive to God throughout the day. How does a person learn how to be attentive to God in the midst of the busyness of life?

2. What can we do at the start of a day to make ourselves attentive to God? What can we do at the end of a day?

3. When do you find it most difficult to be aware of the presence of God? What could you do at these times to increase your consciousness of His presence?

THE DISCIPLINE OF WHOLE-LIFE DISCIPLESHIP

88 – Ordinary Life as a Spiritual Vocation

Reading: Colossians 3:22-4:1

Servant of all, to toil for man	Mark 10:45
Thou didst not, Lord, refuse;	
Thy majesty did not disdain	
To be employed for us.	Phil. 2:7
Son of the carpenter, receive	Matt. 13:55
This humble work of mine;	
Worth to my meanest labor give,	
By joining it to Thine.	1 Cor. 15:58
End of my every action Thou,	1 Cor. 10:31; Col. 3:17
In all things Thee I see;	
Accept my hallowed labor now,	
I do it unto Thee.	Col. 3:23
Thy bright example I pursue,	
To Thee in all things rise;	
And all I think or speak or do	
Is one great sacrifice.	Rom. 12:1
Careless through outward cares I go,	Matt. 6:25
From all distraction free;	
My hands are but engaged below,	
My heart is still with Thee.	Ps. 24:4

CHARLES WESLEY

Reflection Questions:

1. How does this hymn demonstrate the spiritual value of normal work?

2. Explain the meaning of the following lines: 'End of my every action Thou,/In all things Thee I see.' What does it mean to 'see' Jesus in the midst of ordinary tasks?

3. Reread the final stanza. How can we be 'engaged below' while still maintaining an awareness of the presence of Jesus?

89 – Fulfilling the Great Commission

Reading: Matthew 28:16-20

Go, labor on: spend, and be spent,	2 Cor. 12:15
Thy joy to do the Father's will:	John 4:34
It is the way the Master went;	
Should not the servant tread it still?	Matt. 10:24

Go, labor on! 'tis not for naught — Phil. 2:16
Thine earthly loss is heavenly gain;
Men heed thee, love thee, praise thee not;
The Master praises: what are men? — 1 Cor. 4:4

Go, labor on! Your hands are weak, — Isa. 35:3
Your knees are faint, your soul cast down;
Yet falter not; the prize you seek
Is near—a kingdom and a crown. — Phil. 3:14

Go, labor on while it is day: — John 9:4
The world's dark night is hastening on;
Speed, speed thy work, cast sloth away; — Matt. 25:26
It is not thus that souls are won. — Prov. 11:30

Men die in darkness at thy side,
Without a hope to cheer the tomb;
Take up the torch and wave it wide,
The torch that lights time's thickest gloom.

Toil on, faint not, keep watch and pray, — Gal. 6:9
Be wise the erring soul to win; — Col. 4:5
Go forth into the world's highway,
Compel the wanderer to come in. — Luke 14:23

Toil on, and in thy toil rejoice!   Col. 1:29
For toil comes rest, for exile home;
Soon shalt thou hear the Bridegroom's
    voice,   Matt. 25:6
The midnight peal, Behold, I come!   Rev. 22:12-14

HORATIUS BONAR

Reflection Questions:

1. What reasons does the hymn give to 'Go, labor on?'

2. What does it mean to 'spend, and be spent' for the mission of God?

3. How are you affected by the final two lines of the hymn? How should the expectation of Jesus' second coming keep us motivated as servants of God?

6

MEDITATING ON
SPIRITUAL TRIALS

Fifty years ago Tozer wrote, 'The idea that this world is a playground instead of a battleground has now been accepted in practice by the vast majority of Christians.'[1] The statement is truer today than when the ink first dried. Civilization and culture have united to convince Christians that the greatest evil in life is *missing out*. We honestly feel as if we were born with a basic human right to enjoy a fun, healthy, and successful existence. This assumption explains why so many Christians are not just surprised, but scandalized by their suffering. They feel as if God has hidden something in the fine print of His covenant when life takes a painful twist. The message they have chosen to believe is the empty optimism of talk-show therapy – that if you work hard and do your best, the universe will generously reward the efforts. Avoided like potholes is anything the Bible has to say about Fatherly discipline, devilish temptation,

---

1   See A. W. Tozer, *This World: Playground or Battlefield*, p. 5.

the need to mortify sin, or the uphill climb of normal discipleship.

Such naivety is a serious threat to faith. As Christians, we are soldiers, and we need to engage each day with the sobriety and preparedness that is typical of a soldier who knows that combat is imminent. The following hymns are helpful for shaking off the mental fog of a 'playground mentality' and putting on the alertness of a spiritual combatant. They distill some of the hardest truths about the Christian life, but do so in such a way that reminds those with feeble hands and weak knees that the God who summons us into the furnace is also the one who promises, 'I will never leave you nor forsake you' (Deuteronomy 31:6).

The following hymns cover a broad range of topics, including the struggle to find meaning in suffering, spiritual depression, resisting temptation, and the need for watchfulness. Yet, there is a special focus in this set of hymns on preparing Christians for the unique and inevitable trial of dying. The reason for this emphasis is that we live in a culture that does everything it can to ignore one of the most basic facts of human existence, mortality. It is not unusual in the 21st century to find someone well into their sixties who has never come to terms with the truth that 'it is appointed for man to die once, and after that comes judgment' (Hebrews 9:27). The folly of this willed ignorance is obvious. An older generation of believers often spoke of the importance of 'dying well.' In saying this, they were not being morbid. Rather, they understood that death was like a final moment in the Colosseum that no Christian could avoid. Such a climactic moment should not be left to the peripheries of thought. Instead, preparation is needed to make sure that we are ready to cling to the hand of Jesus when our name is called to endure what truly is the darkest hour.

This in mind, the hymns included on death should be viewed as some of the most important spiritual exercises in this book. According to Hebrews 2:14-15, fear of death is one of Satan's chief tactics for subjecting us to a lifetime of slavery. To overcome such fear is to pull back the curtains that darken Christian hope. After all, it is only after we grasp the meaning of Jesus' words 'I have the keys to Death and Hades' (Revelation 1:18) that we can stop idolizing the present moment and begin to live with the joyful awareness that the horizon before us is as vast as eternity itself.

90 – Beneath a Frowning Providence

Reading: Genesis 50:15-21

God moves in a mysterious way	
His wonders to perform;	Rom. 11:33
He plants his footsteps in the sea,	Ps. 77:19
And rides upon the storm.	Ps. 18:10

Deep in unfathomable mines
Of never-failing skill
He treasures up his bright designs,
And works his sov'reign will.   Job 28

Ye fearful saints, fresh courage take;
The clouds ye so much dread
Are big with mercy, and shall break
In blessings on your head.   Isa. 45:8, Hosea 10:12

Judge not the Lord by feeble sense,   2 Cor. 5:7
But trust him for his grace;
Behind a frowning providence   Prov. 3:11-12
He hides a smiling face.

His purposes will ripen fast,   Isa. 55:10
Unfolding ev'ry hour;
The bud may have a bitter taste,
But sweet will be the flow'r.   Ps. 66:10-12

Blind unbelief is sure to err,
And scan his work in vain;
God is his own interpreter,   1 Cor. 2:11
And he will make it plain.[1]

WILLIAM COWPER

---

1   Another hymn that takes up the difficulty of experiencing the chastening hand of a loving Father is James Deck's 'It Is Thy Hand, My God.'

Reflection Questions:

1. Reread the third stanza. Summarize this stanza in your own words.

2. Why is it dangerous to judge our circumstances using 'feeble sense'? What examples are there in the Bible of people being misled due to trusting their senses (particularly their eyes)?

3. Reread the final stanza. What does it mean that 'God is his own interpreter?' How should this truth influence our faith as we walk through suffering?

91 – The Refining Fire of Affliction

Reading: 2 Corinthians 12:7-10

I ask'd the Lord that I might grow	
In faith, and love, and every grace;	
Might more of his salvation know,	
And seek more earnestly his face.	Ps. 27:8

'Twas he who taught me thus to pray,	Jer. 29:13
And he, I trust, has answer'd prayer;	
But it has been in such a way	
As almost drove me to despair.	2 Cor. 1:8

I hoped that in some favour'd hour	
At once he'd answer my request;	
And, by his love's constraining power,	2 Cor. 5:14
Subdue my sins, and give me rest.	Micah 7:19

Instead of this, he made me feel	
The hidden evils of my heart,	Mark 7:19
And let the angry powers of hell	
Assault my soul in every part.	

Yea, more, with his own hand he seem'd
Intent to aggravate my woe;
Cross'd all the fair designs I schem'd,
Blasted my gourds,[1] and laid me low.

"Lord, why is this?" I trembling cry'd,	
"Wilt thou pursue thy worm to death?"	Job 25:6
"'Tis in this way," the Lord reply'd,	
"I answer prayer for grace and faith.	

---

1   A 'gourd' is a large fruit with a hard skin. The image here is of foul weather that ruins anticipated delights.

"These inward trials I employ
"From self, and pride, to set thee free,
"And break thy schemes of earthly joy,
"That thou may'st seek thy all in me."　　2 Cor. 12:7-10

JOHN NEWTON

Reflection Questions:

1. What is the prayer of the speaker at the start of the hymn?

2. What is surprising about how God answers the prayer?

3. What explanation is given at the end of the hymn for why God allows painful trials?

92 – Joy in the Midst of Anxiety

Reading: Habakkuk 3:17-19

Sometimes a light surprises
The Christian while he sings;
It is the Lord, who rises
With healing in his wings; Mal. 4:2
When comforts are declining,
He grants the soul again
A season of clear shining,
To cheer it after rain.

In holy contemplation,
We sweetly then pursue
The theme of God's salvation,
And find it ever new;
Set free from present sorrow,
We cheerfully can say,
"Let the unknown tomorrow
Bring with it what it may." Matt. 6:34

It can bring with it nothing
But he will bear us through;
Who gives the lilies clothing
Will clothe his people too; Matt. 6:28
Beneath the spreading heavens
No creature but is fed; Ps. 145:15
And he who feeds the ravens
Will give his children bread. Ps. 147:9

Though vine nor fig tree neither   Hab. 3:17-18
Their wonted fruit should bear,
Though all the field should wither,
Nor flocks nor herds be there;
Yet God the same abideth,
His praise shall tune my voice,
For, while in him confiding,
I cannot but rejoice.[1]

WILLIAM COWPER

Reflection Questions:

1. Why is the word 'sometimes' important in the first line?

2. The third stanza says, 'It [tomorrow] can bring with it nothing.' What is the meaning of this line? What light does Matthew 6:34 shed on the meaning of this line?

3. The last stanza is largely a paraphrase of Habakkuk 3:17-18. Why does the hymn end with an extended paraphrase of these verses?

---

1   For another incisive hymn on the topic of spiritual anxiety, see 'The Lord Will Happiness Divine' by William Cowper.

93 – The World Is a Battlefield

Reading: Matthew 7:13-14

Believe not those who say	
The upward path is smooth,	Matt. 7:13
Lest thou should stumble in the way,	
And faint before the truth.	Heb. 12:3

It is the only road	
Unto the realms of joy;	
But he who seeks that blest abode	
Must all his powers employ.	1 Tim. 4:10

Arm-arm thee for the fight!	Eph. 6:11
Cast useless loads away;	Heb. 12:1
Watch through the darkest hours of night;	Matt. 26:41
Toil through the hottest day.	Col. 1:29

To labor and to love,	
To pardon and endure,	
To lift thy heart to God above,	
And keep thy conscience pure.	1 Tim. 1:5

Be this thy constant aim,	1 Cor. 9:24
Thy hope, thy chief delight,	
What matter who should whisper blame	
Or who should scorn or slight.	Heb. 12:2

What matters—if God approve,	
And if within thy breast,	
Thou feel the comfort of His love,	
The earnest of His rest?[1]	Heb. 4:1

ANNE BRONTË

---

1   For another hymns on this topic see 'From Trials Unexempted' by Charles Wesley and 'Faint Not Christian!' by J. H. Evans.

Reflection Questions:

1. Why is it important to remember that the Christian life is often a difficult road to follow?

2. How is this hymn a commentary on Jesus' words in Matthew 7:13-14?

3. According to the last stanza, why should we be willing to swim against the current of social norms and popular culture?

94 – Watch and Pray

Reading: Matthew 26:36-56

Christian, seek not yet repose,
Cast thy dreams of ease away;
Thou art in the midst of foes:
Watch and pray.   Matt. 26:41

Principalities and pow'rs,
Must'ring their unseen array,   Eph. 6:12
Wait for thine unguarded hours:
Watch and pray.

Gird thy heav'nly armor on,   Eph. 6:13
Wear it ever, night and day;
Ambushed lies the evil one: 1 Pet. 5:8
Watch and pray.

Hear the victors who o'ercame: Rev. 12:11 KJ
Still they mark each warrior's way;
All with one sweet voice exclaim,
"Watch and pray."

Hear, above all, hear thy Lord,
Him thou lovest to obey;
Hide within thy heart his word,
"Watch and pray."   Rev. 3:2-3

Watch, as if on that alone
Hung the issue of the day;
Pray, that help may be sent down:
Watch and pray.

CHARLOTTE ELLIOT

Reflection Questions:

1. How do you feel after reading this hymn? How would you think differently – and behave differently – if you read this hymn every morning?

2. What does it mean to watch and pray? How does someone continue to watch and pray while going about the normal tasks and responsibilities of life?

3. Reread the final stanza. What does it mean to 'Watch, as if on that alone/Hung the issue of the day?'

95 – How Firm a Foundation

Reading: Isaiah 43:1-3

How firm a foundation, ye saints of the Lord,	Isa. 28:16
Is laid for your faith in His excellent word!	
What more can He say than to you He hath said,	
To you who for refuge to Jesus have fled?	Ps. 62:7

'Fear not, I am with thee, O be not dismayed,
For I am thy God, and will still give thee aid;
I'll strengthen thee, help thee, and cause thee
   to stand,
Upheld by My righteous, omnipotent hand.'   Isa. 41:10

'When through the deep waters I call thee to go,	
The rivers of sorrow shall not overflow;	Isa. 43:2
For I will be with thee, thy troubles to bless,	
And sanctify to thee thy deepest distress.'	Heb. 12:10

'When through fiery trials thy pathway shall lie,	
My grace, all sufficient, shall be thy supply;	Isa. 43:2
The flame shall not hurt thee; I only design	
Thy dross to consume, and thy gold to refine.'	1 Pet. 1:7

'E'en down to old age all My people shall prove	Isa. 46:4
My sovereign, eternal, unchangeable love;	
And then, when grey hairs shall their temples adorn,	Ps. 71:18
Like lambs they shall still in My bosom be borne.'	Isa. 40:11

'The soul that on Jesus hath leaned for repose,	John 13:23
I will not, I will not desert to his foes;	
That soul, though all hell should endeavor to shake,	Luke 22:31
I'll never, no, never, no, never forsake!'	Deut. 31:6, Heb. 13:5

Anonymous

Reflection Questions:

1. This hymn makes a lot of use of God speaking in the first person ('I' and 'My'). How does this literary device contribute to the message of this hymn?

2. How can we remind ourselves in the midst of 'deep waters' and 'fiery trials' that God is with us?

3. This hymn is about laying a 'firm foundation' for our faith. How does this hymn encourage us to trust in God in the midst of difficult circumstances?

96 – To Live Is Christ, to Die Is Gain

Reading: Philippians 1:19-30

Lord, it belongs not to my care
Whether I die or live; Phil. 1:21
To love and serve Thee is my share,
And this Thy grace must give.

If life be long, I will be glad
That I may long obey;
If short, yet why should I be sad 2 Cor. 5:8-9
To soar to endless day? Rev. 21:23

Christ leads me through no darker rooms
Than He went through before; Heb. 5:8-9
No one into His kingdom comes,
But through His open'd door. John 10:7

Come, Lord, when grace has made me meet
Thy blesséd face to see; 1 John 3:3
For if Thy work on earth be sweet,
What will Thy glory be!

Then I shall end my sad complaints,
And weary, sinful days,
And join with all triumphant saints
Who sing my Jehovah's praise. Heb. 12:23

My knowledge of that life is small;
The eye of faith is dim; 1 Cor. 13:12
But 'tis enough that Christ knows all,
And I shall be with Him. John 14:13

RICHARD BAXTER

Reflection Questions:

1. What does it mean that 'Christ leads me through no darker rooms/Than He went through before?'

2. What did Paul mean when he said, 'To live is Christ, and to die is gain' (Philippians 1:21)? How is this attitude reflected in this hymn?

3. A child-like faith is displayed in the final stanza. Why is such child-like faith needed as we journey through life?

97 – Forever with the Lord

Reading: 2 Corinthians 5:1-8

Forever with the Lord!	1 Thess. 4:17
Amen! so let it be.	
Life from the dead is in that word,	Ps. 119:50
'Tis immortality.	
Here in the body pent,[1]	2 Cor. 5:1-4
Absent from Him, I roam,	2 Cor. 5:6
Yet nightly pitch my moving tent	
A day's march nearer home.	
My Father's house on high,	
Home of my soul, how near	
At times to faith's foreseeing eye	
Thy golden gates appear!	Rev. 21:21
Ah, then my spirit faints	
To reach the land I love,	
The bright inheritance of saints,	
Jerusalem above!	Rev. 21:2, Gal. 4:26
Forever with the Lord!	
O Father, 'tis Thy will.	
The promise of that faithful word	
E'en here to me fulfil.	
Be Thou at my right hand,	Ps. 16:8
Then can I never fail.	
Uphold Thou me, and I shall stand;	Isa. 41:10
Fight Thou, and I'll prevail.	Ps. 35:1

---

1   Some Christians may be uncomfortable with the idea that we are somehow trapped in the body. Yet, we need to remember that our present bodies often suffer pain and discomfort. Did not Paul himself – the great preacher of the resurrection – say, 'It is better to be absent from the body and to be present with the Lord' (2 Cor. 5:8 NKJ)?

So when my dying breath
Shall set my spirit free,   Heb. 12:23
By death I shall escape from death   1 Cor. 15:36
To endless life with Thee.

Knowing as I am known;   1 Cor. 13:12
How shall I love that word
And oft repeat before the throne,
"Forever with the Lord!"

JAMES MONTGOMERY

Reflection Questions:

1. The hymn begins and ends with the same line. Why is this?

2. As we age we often feel as if each day is another step toward death. How does the second stanza flip this attitude?

3. The hymn says, 'By death I shall escape from death.' What does this statement mean? See John 5:24 for additional insight.

98 – Death: the Last Battle

Reading: Hebrews 2:14-18

Abide with me: fast falls the eventide;	Luke 24:29

Abide with me: fast falls the eventide;   Luke 24:29
The darkness deepens; Lord, with me abide.
When other helpers fail and comforts flee,
Help of the helpless, abide with me.

Swift to its close ebbs out life's little day;   Job 7:6
Earth's joys grow dim, its glories pass away.
Change and decay in all around I see.
O thou who changest not, abide with me.   Lam. 3:23

I need thy presence every passing hour.
What but thy grace can foil the tempter's
   power?   Heb. 2:18
Who like thyself my guide and strength
   can be?
Through cloud and sunshine, O abide with me.

I fear no foe with thee at hand to bless,
Ills have no weight, and tears no bitterness.
Where is death's sting? Where, grave, thy
   victory?   1 Cor. 15:55
I triumph still, if thou abide with me.

Hold thou thy cross before my closing eyes.
Shine through the gloom and point me to
   the skies.
Heaven's morning breaks and earth's vain
   shadows flee;   Song 2:17
In life, in death, O Lord, abide with me.[1]   Rev. 1:18

Henry Francis Lyte

---

1   Anyone who has not yet come to terms with the seriousness of death should reflect on 'There Is an Hour' by Andrew Reed.

Reflection Questions:

1. The hymn begins with a reference to Luke 24:29. Why does the hymn refer to this text?

2. Christians often say that they do not fear death itself, but they do fear the process of dying. How does this hymn talk honestly about the spiritual combat involved in the process of dying?

3. It is easy to overlook just how profound the final line of the hymn is. Why is it so remarkable that Jesus is able to abide with us *in death*?

99 – *The Hope of Bodily Resurrection*

Reading: 1 Corinthians 15:35-49

And must this Body die?
This well wrought Frame decay?
And must these active Limbs of mine
Lie mould'ring in the Clay?

Corruption, Earth and Worms
Shall but refine this flesh,
Till my triumphant Spirit comes
To put it on afresh.   1 Cor. 15:42-44

God my Redeemer lives,   Job 19:25
And often from the Skies
Looks down, and watches all my Dust,
Till he shall bid it rise.

Array'd in glorious Grace
Shall these vile Bodies shine,   1 Cor. 15:43
And every Shape and every Face,
Be heavenly and divine.

These lively Hopes we owe   1 Pet. 1:3
Lord, to thy dying Love;
We would adore thy Grace below,
And sing thy Power above.

Savior accept the Praise
Of these our humble Songs,
Till Tunes of nobler Sound we raise
With our immortal Tongues.   2 Cor. 5:4

Isaac Watts

Reflection Questions:

1. Why do you think the first stanza begins with three questions? Why is the death of the body such a difficult truth to accept?

2. What does it mean that our resurrected bodies will be 'Array'd in glorious Grace'? How will these bodies be the same as our mortal bodies? How will they be different?

3. A lot of Christians imagine that our eternal condition will be more like that of a ghost, or of an angel, than that of an embodied human being. How does this hymn correct this common misconception?

100 – The Land of Pure Delight

Reading: Revelation 21

There is a Land of pure Delight,
Where Saints immortal reign;   Rev. 20:6
Infinite Day excludes the Night,   Rev. 22:5
And Pleasures banish Pain.   Rev. 21:4

There everlasting Spring abides,   Rev. 22:2
And never with'ring Flow'rs;
Death like a narrow Sea, divides   Rev. 21:1
This heav'nly Land from ours.

Sweet Fields beyond the swelling Flood,
Stand drest in living Green;
So to the Jews old Canaan stood,
While Jordan roll'd between.   Josh. 1:11

But tim'rous[1] Mortals start and shrink,
To cross the narrow Sea;
And linger, shiv'ring on the Brink,
And fear to launch away.

O could we make our Doubts remove,
Those gloomy Doubts that rise,
And see the Cana'n that we love,
With unbeclouded Eyes.

Could we but climb where Moses stood,   Num. 27:12
And view the Landscape o'er,
Not Jordan's Stream, nor Death's cold
    Flood,
Should fright us from the Shore.

ISAAC WATTS

---

1   Fearful.

Reflection Questions:

1. How does this hymn use the position of the Israelites beside the Jordan River to help us understand our spiritual condition?

2. The final three stanzas are very honest about the way in which we 'linger, shiv'ring on the Brink' of eternal life. What is the cause of such fear?

3. According to the final stanza, what perspective do we need in order to overcome our fear of death? How do the first three stanzas try to shift our perspective?

Final Lap: The Joy of Eternal Life

Reading: Song of Solomon 2:10-13

> *The sands of time are sinking,*
> *The dawn of heaven breaks,*
> *The summer morn I've sighed for,*
> *The fair sweet morn awakes;*
> *Dark, dark hath been the midnight,*
> *But dayspring is at hand,*
> *And glory, glory dwelleth*
> *In Emmanuel's land.*
>
> *The King there in his beauty*
> *Without a veil is seen;*
> *It were a well-spent journey,*
> *Though sev'n deaths lay between:*
> *The Lamb with his fair army*
> *Doth on Mount Zion stand,*
> *And glory, glory dwelleth*
> *In Emmanuel's land.*
>
> *O Christ, he is the fountain,*
> *The deep sweet well of love!*
> *The streams on earth I've tasted,*
> *More deep I'll drink above:*
> *There to an ocean fullness*
> *His mercy doth expand,*
> *And glory, glory dwelleth*
> *In Emmanuel's land.*

The bride eyes not her garment,
But her dear bridegroom's face;
I will not gaze at glory,
But on my King of grace;
Not at the crown he gifteth,
But on his piercèd hand:
The Lamb is all the glory
Of Emmanuel's land.

SAMUEL RUTHERFORD AND A. R. COUSIN